CLOSE TO THE GROUND

reflections on the
seven factors of enlightenment

Geri Larkin

Sᴀᴍʙʜᴀʟᴀ

BOULDER   2013

Shambhala Publications, Inc.
4720 Walnut Street
Boulder, Colorado 80301
www.shambhala.com

A Rodmell Press book

Cover collage created by Gopa & Ted2, Inc., based on photographs from Getty Images.

Printed in the United States of America

⊗ This edition is printed on acid-free paper that meets the American National Standards Institute Z39.48 Standard.
♻ Shambhala Publications makes every effort to print on recycled paper. For more information please visit www.shambhala.com.
Shambhala Publications is distributed worldwide by
Penguin Random House, Inc., and its subsidiaries.

Editors: Holly Hammond, Linda Cogozzo
Design: Gopa & Ted2, Inc.
Indexer: Ty Koontz
Author Photo: Jeffrey Ericson Allen

Library of Congress Cataloging-in-Publication Data
Larkin, Geri, author.
Close to the ground: reflections on the seven factors of enlightenment / Geri Larkin. First edition. Berkeley, California: Rodmell Press, 2013.
    xi, 177 pages; 23 cm
    BQ4398 .L37 2013
    ISBN 9781930485341 (pbk.)

CLOSE TO THE GROUND

Praise for *Close to the Ground*

Part memoir, part philosophy, Geri Larkin's new book invites us all to explore the seven factors of enlightenment from the ground of our own splendid lives. Larkin's storytelling sparkles with the down-to-earth honesty, wisdom, and good humor that can only come from a lifetime of committed practice.

— Charlotte Bell, author of *Yoga for Meditators*
and *Mindful Yoga, Mindful Life*

With humor and warmth grounded in decades of Zen Buddhist practice, Geri Larkin offers a fresh perspective on this timeless, core teaching of Buddhism. *Close to the Ground* invites readers to discover the awakened heart that's available in each and every moment of our often wonderfully chaotic lives. Highly recommended.

— Vince Cousino Anila, Guiding Teacher
Still Point Zen Buddhist Temple

This wonderful book can serve as a great encouragement to one's practice. Geri Larkin, a longtime Zen practitioner and teacher, seamlessly weaves together various strands of Buddhist teaching. Using as chapter headings the seven factors of enlightenment, a practice schema usually associated with the Theravadin Vipassana tradition, she skillfully integrates Zen stories, anecdotes from the Buddha's life, and examples from her own training and practice to clearly reveal what spiritual practice is about. Highly recommended!

— Richard Shrobe, author of
Elegant Failure: A Guide to Zen Koans

When I studied Zen under Geri Larkin at Still Point in Detroit, I often thought that books couldn't do what a real teacher does. A book doesn't correct your posture when you're slouching; a book doesn't notice when you get lazy and remind you to get up in the morning; a book doesn't correct you when you speak carelessly. But now she has written a book that accepts no excuses, that tells you tirelessly why the world needs the dharma, and why the practice will change the world if we are committed to it. This book can be the angel on your shoulder, giving you the reminders you need.

— Bija Andrew Wright, Buddhist teacher
and blogger at www.zenbija.com

This book is dedicated to Kassapa, in gratitude
for his unfailing encouragement to continue writing
years after I thought I was done.

Contents

Thank Yous

FIRST TO Linda and Donald at Rodmell Press. Thank you to you and your colleagues for even existing in this time of publishing turmoil. And for your effort to keep Buddhist teachings alive. A huge bow. Thank you to my dharma family, to my bloodline family, and to my family of friends. Without you there are no stories, no lessons. Thank you to Jeffrey Ericson Allen, composer extraordinaire, Monkey the Cat, and Bodhi the Dog for sharing Laughing Moon Hermitage, such as it is. Thank you to Samu Sunim and Haju Sunim for getting me started even as I kicked and screamed. Finally, unending bows to Zen Master Ji Bong Sunim. Every day I bow in gratitude for your friendship and unerring guidance.

Introduction

What is the purpose of our practice?
It is to cultivate meditation and wisdom together, . . .
If anyone . . . wishes to join us,
We will welcome them,
Whether they be a monk or a lay person,
Whether one is male or female,
Whether one is old or young,
Whether one is wise or foolish,
Whether one is noble or mean,
Whether one is friendly or aloof,
Whether one is in accord with us or against us.
—ZEN MASTER GYEONGHEO SEONGU

A FEW YEARS BACK, in one of Oregon's coldest and wettest winters, I moved from a fancy-pants studio apartment in Portland's Pearl District to half of an unfinished garage in Eugene. The broken-heart saga that was mine is too trite to repeat here. The garage space was slightly bigger than a truck, front to back and side to side. I had a table, two chairs, a mattress, and a set of teacups that my friend Tina gave me. There was a dorm room fridge and a hot plate. Two space heaters didn't keep me warm on the days when wind blew through three sides of each of the garage doors. I had no job and no savings I could tap. On the other hand, the car worked and Bodhi the Dog loved me. It's the closest I've ever come to being a living hologram of a country western song.

After the initial shock of finding myself in the situation I had made for myself, I was happy. Even with a broken heart I was happy. This happiness wasn't the "Oh my God, he called me!" happiness or even the "I just got the raise I was hoping for" version. Instead the feeling was more like a deep and abiding okayness with everything just the way it was. It was an okayness so deep that all of the melodrama that I had gone through to land in the garage felt more like bubbles on the surface of deep ocean waves than anything else. I wish I was poetic so I could describe the feeling more fully. Hopefully you'll get the idea anyway.

The thing is I wasn't happy because I was young and healthy with my whole life ahead of me. I haven't been young for thirty years. And while I'm mostly healthy, these knees are done running. Happiness wasn't coming from any thing. It just was.

Considering this, years later, I've realized that a quarter century of regular meditation practice is a big part of the why. Also knowing how to live like a monk from years of temple life, mostly as a guiding teacher at Still Point Zen Buddhist Temple in Detroit, probably counts for something. But it's more than that. How I've practiced seems to be a key reason for this stream of happy that doesn't show signs of letting up any time soon. For some reason, nagging parents maybe, I've always given everything I've done my best effort, including meditation practice. Sometimes this has led to kudos in the world of business. And sometimes it has led to just-this-side-of a homeless life as a monk. Along the way, I've had great fun, which has in turn led to not taking this life too seriously or personally. I've learned, sometimes the hard way, that paying attention is a gate to satisfying relationships, creativity, and gratitude with a big G. Throw in innate curiosity, and happiness has been mine, whatever the circumstance.

To tell you the truth, I've never thought about any of these things all that much. But then, a few months ago, I read an old teaching in Buddhism's early Pali Canon that listed the seven factors of enlightenment. Included were: mindfulness, the investigation of phenomena, energetic effort, ease, joy, concentration, and equanimity. Staring at them, I couldn't believe how clear and simple a formula they were for falling into a sweet juicy life no matter the situation we find ourselves swimming through. And my own little dust mote of a life, including the garage *kalpa*, was living proof they work.

MINDFULNESS

If you spend any time in the world of Zen, you will hear a joke about a student climbing a mountain three separate times to ask his teacher for advice only to hear the same response each time: "Pay attention!" We don't, you know. Instead, these days, the majority of us skim the surfaces of our lives, missing most of what is going on. The Buddha taught that if a person is truly mindful, enlightenment will be hers in fifteen days. I have yet to hear of a person who has been mindful enough for that to happen. I try hard and still trip over my own shoes in the middle of the hallway on a regular basis.

INVESTIGATION OF PHENOMENA

Investigation of phenomena is a permanent get-out-of-boredom-hell-free card. It turns out that curiosity about ourselves and the world in which we find ourselves is a powerful spiritual practice, especially when one question leads to another. Just asking ourselves, "Is what I think really true?" can clean out all sorts of karmic gunk that has been holding us back. "What is amazing about this?" is another question that has the capacity to pull us into right now in an open-hearted way. I've yet to be in a situation that wasn't amazing in some way, including the conversation I had with a young—nineteen maybe—deli woman this morning at the local grocery store. It turns out that she has pulled herself up and out of some serious dreck and managed to find herself a full-time job that will house and feed her while she sorts her life out. Given the story of what she has had to do to pull this off, ranging from homelessness to taking her own father to court, her genuine cheerfulness was, in a word, amazing. The day has gone uphill from there. A windstorm that sounds exactly like a sound track from a cheap zombie movie. Monkey the Cat's unwavering persistence when she decided that it was time for a treat. The soft smell from this morning's incense sneaking around corners of the hermitage. Nonstop phenomena, just crying out for some investigation.

ENERGETIC EFFORT

Energetic effort is so important to a spiritual life that it is its own *paramita*, or "heavenly skill." When I refuse to make excuses for not doing just about any kind of chore and just do it, I can't get over how pleasurable it can be. This includes scrubbing toilets by hand. On the hottest Friday of last summer I offered to help spread thirty (30!) huge sacks of wet (!) hemlock bark all over the yard in an effort to cut back on the need for watering. We're talking two full carloads of heavy—as in a sleeping-three-year-old-child heavy—bags of mulch. I just made the yard a pretend gym and named myself coach. Moving the bags from Ace Hardware to the backyard took hours less than I thought it would, and when the job was done it felt like finishing a half marathon. The runner's high lasted for hours.

EASE

The *Oxford American Dictionary* defines *ease* as freedom from pain, trouble, or anxiety. I had the good fortune to visit the Emilia-Romagna region of Italy back when the slow food movement was starting to take hold. Evening meals were hours long. Sometimes five. No matter who I was with and no matter where we ate, we were going to have a meal with as many parts as I have dishes in my cupboard. And it was going to take its own sweet time. People relaxed, sipped wine, told stories, and laughed. We got to know each other as individuals with multifaceted lives, fascinating ones. To this day, they were the best meals of my life, meals where we simply enjoyed the passing of time together.

JOY

Joy, as opposed to pleasure, is that sweet feeling that everything is okay. Happy extreme, it feels like the ether of a life lived mindfully and with curiosity. Each one of us has her own formula. Surrounding ourselves with natural beauty, painting a still life, or simply catching a glimpse of a religious statue can trigger a feeling of quiet joy. So can meditation. In this stage of life, where five hours of sleep appears to be the norm, a night of seven or eight hours can lead to delirious joy.

CONCENTRATION

Concentration, or mindfulness aimed at a specific task, like making a new recipe, learning a new piano piece, or closely following our breath when we meditate, adds additional fuel to a deepening happiness.

EQUANIMITY

Equanimity is defined as a calmness of mind or temper. Like concentration, equanimity, especially when it takes the form of letting go of something we might want to grasp, feeds happiness. Every time. Everything (everything!) comes and goes in life. When we stop fighting this truth, equanimity becomes possible.

For three years now I've mined these seven factors of enlightenment for dharma talks and essays. Every time I've come back to the list I've wished that there was some book out there that used these factors to share how we can each live a life of great awakening without needing any more than what is right in front of us moment by moment. When I couldn't find one, I decided to write it. May Lord Buddha have my back.

Close to the Ground has seven sections, each one reflecting an enlightenment factor. Within each section you'll find a half dozen dharma talks that consider some aspect or aspects of the factor. For examples of teachings that are pertinent to the topic, I've mostly mined the Pali Canon, the collection of texts regarded by many Buddhists as the word of the Buddha (*Buddha vacana*). Taken together, his teachings are direct, thorough, and uncompromising for a time when our world can feel indirect, piecemeal, and confused. Within the canon I've mostly tapped the Digha Nikaya discourses because they seem to be aimed at laypeople as much as monks and nuns. May the stories and teachings be entertaining and helpful. May they lead to your feeling a great okayness with your own life. And may you use that life to help others.

1: Mindfulness

Just as a ray continues out from one point to another to make a straight line, how you keep your mind in this very moment makes your whole life. Many people only follow their thinking, their desire, anger, and ignorance. So they get suffering in situation after situation. But if you wake up, right now, you get happiness. Which one do you like? The name for this "wakeup" is sometimes called paying attention. The Buddha called it Right Mindfulness. —ZEN MASTER SEUNG SAHN[1]

BEAU EXPLORES A LADYBUG

MY GRANDSON, BEAU, shows up at the door pouting. His nap was cut short, and he has no interest in "peeing like a big boy" before we head for the park. He's dressed in not one but three superhero accessories: a Superman cape, a Spiderman suit, and a Darth Vader helmet. They aren't protecting him from his mood.

When we get to the park ten minutes later, he walks slowly, head down. I give him room to wrestle with his almost-three-year-old thoughts. Suddenly he shouts, "Look!"

A ladybug has landed on his hand.

We can't believe it.

It turns out I know quite a bit about ladybugs. I know they love to eat aphids, the mean girls of all things gardening. I know they are really beetles and that they smell through their feet and chew side to side. They touch, smell, and taste through their antennae and can play dead if they think you are a predator.

The bug on Beau's hand is playing dead. As I spout off all my instafacts Beau ignores me completely. Instead he just stares at the ladybug, silenced. I stare with him. We quietly notice her big black spots and her bright red wing covers and the teeny little see-through wings peeking out just under the covers. We see her scary pincher mouth and her tiny little legs that look like they have been whittled out of micro matchsticks.

After a while, maybe five minutes, she decides that the two gods staring her down are probably safe and flies off. Watching her, we look up just in time to see a leaf fall from the tree over our heads. It is Tinkerbell dancing, catching the light sometimes and looking like it is getting ready to do a flip, just before it actually does. We are enchanted.

As we stare I think about how every dharma teacher I have ever known has emphasized mindfulness over just about anything else. Pay attention to your breath! Pay attention to your mantra! Pay attention to your koan! Keep going back to it over and over and over—don't stray. The Buddha was first in line with this admonishing. In the Samyutta Nikaya he instructs: "And what, monks, is right mindfulness? Here, monks, a monk dwells contemplating the body in the body, ardent, clearly comprehending, mindful, having removed longing and dejection in regard to the world. He dwells contemplating feelings in feelings . . . . mind in mind . . . . [and] phenomena in phenomena, ardent, clearly comprehending, mindful, having removed longing and dejection in regard to the world. This is called right mindfulness."[2]

That I got lost in paying attention to the ladybug and the leaf is probably the result of twenty-five years of determined spiritual practice. That Beau was just as lost comes from the purity of his life experience so far. He doesn't know how not to pay attention.

It's hard not to be jealous.

When the leaf finally lands, Beau grins at me and takes off running as fast as he can with his arms wide open. He is happiness personified. No, he is more than that. He is splendid. It is a splendidness that grows out of a feeling of inherent okayness with all that is. In the Tibetan tradition such splendidness is considered to be a form of bravery and sits right up there with four other categories of spiritual warriorship: being free of deceptions through awareness of habitual patterns; jumping into the freedom of right now; seeing the sacredness of all things, sentient and nonsentient; and synchronizing our bodies and minds. Sakyong Mipham, a much-venerated Tibetan teacher, explains it this way: "Splendidness is a physical expression as well as a psychological one—the result of bravery in relationship to our physical being. Meditating with our whole body increases our realization. Eating in a balanced way brings energy. Moving energizes us. . . . Through bravery, we are fully activating our vitality. . . . Therefore we wholeheartedly embody every aspect of our physical domain."[3]

Tibetan Buddhism has a perfect word to describe Beau: *ziji*. Ziji refers to a person's aliveness and how it gives off an aura of bright-ness and vitality. Think rainbow-colored halo.

Beau trips, falls on all fours, and jumps up before I can get to him. We look at each other and laugh until we both start hiccupping. Then he reaches for my hand and we go back to the River Walk. When I look down at his little fingers I swear they are glowing.

FEAR AS A BEST FRIEND

I once lived with a man who was known for his fearlessness. He was a genuine outdoorsman, the kind who climbs cliffs with his hands and knows how to live in a tiny unheated log cabin with-out running water somewhere near the Artic Circle. He was fear-less—except for one thing. The sight of a spider, even an adorable little common house spider, would turn him to mush. He taught me that everyone, everyone, is afraid of something. We all have things that frighten us. Even Buddha, prior to his enlightenment, had bouts with just-this-side-of-passing-out fear. One time he was meditating by himself in the forest at night. This was during his six-year ascetic period. He saw something that looked like a snake. That did it. He was so terrified that he sat unmoving for hours until morning, when he discovered that his snake was simply a piece of rope. "The loneliness of the forest is hard to bear, it is hard to take pleasure in being alone. . . . When at night I stayed in such fright-ening and fearful places, and an animal passed by, or a peacock broke a twig, or the wind rustled among the leaves, I was filled with terror and panic."[4]

I know that fear. In 1999 I went on a pilgrimage to South Korea with my root teacher, Samu Sunim, and my dharma sister Haju

Linda Murray. To say that the pilgrimage was difficult doesn't even begin to describe the experience. We were true wanderers, with only a second set of robes in backpacks that we carried to something like sixteen temples in less than a month. We climbed mountains, chased down public transportation when we could, and got socked in by a typhoon at one mountain cave hermitage. You would think that we would be scared sometimes.

I was. Twice. Once was when we almost got stuck as we rode in a tiny open metal box straight up the side of one of the Chiri mountains. I had the guts to look down once. When I did, it was clear that we would all die if the box stopped anywhere on the ride up. There wasn't anything that would catch our fall. It was all I could do to keep breathing. And even though Sunim said nothing about the ride, the next morning we hiked down the mountain, taking all day, rather than ride in the box again.

The second time I was all by myself. We were staying in a little temple high up in the mountains, mostly above the tree line. The bathrooms—outhouses—were pretty far away from the buildings, maybe half a football field away. To get there you had to walk up a narrow path with a few stone steps. There was no lighting, and the monks had warned us about poisonous snakes, especially around the bathrooms.

I had a tiny flashlight. One night, as I was carefully making my way back to my bedroom at about 2 a.m., Sunim was walking up the path toward me. When I offered him my flashlight, he just barked, "Turn it off!" So I did and was instantly surrounded by night sounds and rustling. It took what felt like hours to make it all the way back to the little bedroom. By then I was so wide awake I thought my eyes might pop right out of my head. Terror can do that. With nothing better to do, I meditated on the rocks outside our door and discovered that the energy of fear makes for terrific, focused meditation practice. It was one of the clearest sittings I've ever experienced, before or since. My koan, "What is it?" surfaced effortlessly and stayed put for several hours without a break. Then, quiet, quiet. Getting up for formal meditation with everyone else, I was completely refreshed, wide awake, and even happy in my filthy, smelly robes.

I learned a lot on that pilgrimage. Because we were completely dependent on Sunim and his ever-changing itinerary I couldn't escape anything. Even fear. What I realized was that fear isn't something to run away from. The mountain taught me that it only gets worse when we do, or even try to. Instead staring it in the face and then climbing into its mouth turns it into a friendly little house spider instead of the funnel webs your mother always warned you about. Even better, fear offers up an energy that, when embraced rather than resisted, helps us to stay focused on what is right in front of us. It clears out the gunk, if you will. So, while I for one don't go looking for fear, I don't try to run away from it, either. If and when it surfaces, which is rare these days, I simply ask myself if there is something that the fear is telling me to pay attention to. The answer is always yes. And there is always something that I've been ignoring or putting off that needs doing. Every time. So, I just do whatever it is. Every once in a while I realize that the fear is simply an outgrowth of my most excellent imagination. In those cases I use the energy to undergird mindfulness, first in my meditation, and then as I move through the day—until it naturally evaporates.

I try not to miss it.

The Fire of Attention

The woman at the table next to me looks over and asks me what I'm drinking. It's pretty obvious. We're at the Metropol Bakery in Eugene. I have a coffee cup in front of me, filled with dark, chocolate-colored local brew. It smells like freshly roasted coffee beans, which is why I buy it—the smell.

I look at her closely and smile. She is pretty, maybe thirty-five, dressed in the northwest winter uniform of running shoes, jeans, and a rain jacket. Something is a little off though. I can't quite put my finger on what it is. "It's coffee," I tell her.

"Do you drink it all the time?"

I start to say no, that I'm a tea drinker, but the truth is that I have been drinking some form of coffee every day of late.

"Not all the time, but mostly."

"Why?"

"I like to drink it when I'm studying or writing. I like how hot it is. And the smell."

"What are you writing?"

A column for a magazine, I tell her. She proceeds to talk about how lucky I am—true—and how she would love to write for a magazine but she had a terrible accident in college and is still healing.

"Brain damage."

Now I get it. Little things. Her smile is a bit lopsided, and she takes an extra moment to register my responses to her questions. When she asks me questions, she looks me straight in the eye and then leans back, willing to wait for a response. After a few minutes of chit chat, her companion brings her a mocha. By then we know each other's names and have become start-up friends. We nod at each other, and I go back to my notebook. Watching her a little out of the corner of my eye, I see that her movements are very careful. Her concentration is palpable. She picks up her coffee mug carefully, carefully, and sips. Puts it downs as carefully. Then the next sip, attended to just as meticulously.

I am witnessing the fire of attention.

I have a son who loves fire. His discovery of the power of a lit match to ignite newspaper, wood, cloth, leaves, and my exam papers still tops his great-moments list. I suspect that this love came from me. From the age of five I've adored fire in any form. I've stared into thousands of fires and even purchased several piece-of-garbage houses just because a fireplace was included. The place could be—and one was—falling down around itself, but as long as I could make a fire in the fireplace, it was all good. Fire is such a central component in all of our lives that I'm always surprised that we don't honor it more. I for one would be thrilled to have a permanent minisized Olympic torch lit in perpetuity in our tiny side yard. Fire has meant that we've all made it this far, in spite of ourselves. It is a central player in all the creation myths that I can think of. Altars invariably include some form of fire, typically in the form of lit candles. Even with all the technology that drives our todays, it is hard to say no to an old-fashioned barbeque. If you haven't tasted freshly grilled peppers and corn, you have missed two food greats.

Ideas grow out of fire watching. There is just something about the intensity—and warmth—that can make us feel at once comforted and simultaneously open to new thoughts and ideas. At the same time, if my son has taught me anything, it is that fires need to be watched carefully if they are going to stay in the realm of safe. Not just watched, but constantly watched. Because earlier people seemed to understand this need for attention based on their own life experiences, in the Buddhist tradition, Shakyamuni Buddha often used the image of fire in his teachings. He told his followers to practice as though their heads were on fire. Over time his instructions have become an expression still used by many of us who call ourselves teachers to encourage ourselves, and our students, to really dig into our meditation practice. This fire energy is the energy that feeds an unbridled attention, the kind of attention where not much goes unnoticed in our moment-to-moment life.

When as beginning meditators we actually pay attention to our thinking, the news isn't good. Scattered doesn't even start to describe what we discover. I spent years watching two or three levels of thinking that managed to fill my mind at the same time. Once I noticed them, I saw that these ticker tapes of words meant that I was missing out on what was actually going on in my life. I was either planning or worrying, all while a low-level humming of the last song I'd heard on the radio provided a colorful wallpaper for the frenzied thinking. And this was in the days before coffee. I knew that meditation meant watching one's thoughts, but when I really started to pay attention to everything that was going on it made me dizzy. This lasted, ironically, until I put some genuine energy into my practice. As stupid as this sounds, I'll write it anyway. I pretended that my head was on fire.

The results happened fast. The fire of attention led to one-pointed concentration. Two of the ticker-tape tracks dropped away quickly. The third one took longer, dissipating—over time—into a quietness. These days I still get flotsam and jetsam. But now these thoughts don't stick, and they are more and more the exception. What made the fire of attention start to take hold was my deciding to genuinely focus on what my root teacher, Samu Sunim, called the bright moon mind spot, a spot on the floor about a foot and a half in front of where my legs crossed when I sat on a meditation cushion. I was determined to keep my focus on that spot, not to ignore the thinking, but to stay focused on the spot. Over time the bright moon concept dropped away on its own, leaving quiet concentration in its wake. These days I still begin a sitting focused on the ground because it triggers what has finally (finally!) become a habituated intention to practice with the fire of attention.

This form of attention brings surprise gifts with it. One is the experience of vibrations of energy. We can actually experience, for ourselves, how our "solid" bodies are really just a pile-up of vibrations. As S.N. Goenka has expressed it, "The ultimate truth of mind and mental contents is that they are also mere vibration. All mind and matter are mere vibration."[5] A second gift is the experience of recognizing how quickly everything changes, starting with our own thoughts. It's incredible, this arising and passing away. This means—gift three—that we get to shift how we experience life moment by moment. We realize (maybe you won't see this as a gift—sorry) that we are choosing to be angry when we're angry, or sad when we're sad. We can watch how we make mountains out of molehills, without any help from anyone. And we can see how important our initial contact is with someone or something, how it can trigger a parade of reactions, sometimes leading to more of whatever it is, sometimes leading to wanting less, or even occasionally leading to a neutral reaction.

The fire of attention makes it possible for miracles to happen. As just one example, we may discover that we are able to simply watch negative sensations without the knee-jerk reactions we've all come to know and love. In this place we can stop ill will and anger in their tracks by letting their energy die natural deaths. We begin to acknowledge that, in life, we have two jobs, if you will. On the one hand we have the job of genuinely seeing and then working with the inside us—our internal reactions to what we see, smell, taste, and touch. Our outside job then becomes that of figuring out how to work with the increasing understanding of our internal thought patterns. When we accept the jobs, the Buddha's first teaching becomes our north star—the one where he promises that even though our suffering comes out of our own craving, we can use our own lives as our path out of suffering. Zen Master Seung Sahn put it this way: "If your mind is clear, the whole universe is clear. If your mind is not clear, the whole universe is not clear. That is a very important point. So doing strong meditation is important. Having a good sitting practice is very, very important. But the most important point of all this is cutting off all attachment to thinking and return to your before-thinking mind."[6]

We replace greed with generosity. Instead of anger, compassion and loving-kindness take up more of our days. Instead of the delusion that the world revolves around us, we understand more fully how what we think of as ourselves is simply a ball of vibrations that just happens to have our name stamped on it. Decisions shift, relationships shift, and we get to make new friends in coffee shops.

UNITASKING

The Blessed One said to the Venerable Sariputta,
"What now, Sariputta, is a factor for stream-entry?"

"Association with superior persons, venerable sir, is a factor
for stream-entry. Hearing the true Dhamma is a factor for stream-
entry. Careful attention is a factor for stream-entry."[7]

I am sitting at a stop light in downtown Eugene. When I look over my shoulder to my right, I see the woman in the car next to me texting. I think that's illegal these days. Then, as if that isn't enough, she starts penciling in her eyebrows. I stare for a second, partly because I'm a gape queen and partly because I just can't believe she is doing so many things instead of paying attention to the road. The light changes. I drive on and glance back. She is still sitting there, only now the man driving the pickup truck behind her is beeping his brains out. Not a great moment for the civilized world.

Back when I was a management consultant, last century, I remember rewarding multitasking in both myself and others. If I could check emails while I opened my mail, I'd get home sooner. If staff scanned internal memos while they were cruising the Internet for business topics relative to our projects, fine by me.

It turns out that multitasking is a big mistake. According to Michael Komie, a psychologist who consults with executives on work effectiveness, "The research shows that for the average worker in the workplace, multitasking while trying to solve a complex problem is a very bad strategy."[8]

The trouble is that most of us have multitasked for so long now that it can be incredibly hard to back up to one thing at a time. The news gets worse. It turns out that one thing at a time is the *only* portal to waking up. We can't multitask ourselves from here to there. Believe me, I've tried.

What to do?

It helps to know why we want to do several things at once: drive, text, eyebrow fill. Except for those of us who multitask to run away from anxiety or depression or have some form of attention deficit disorder, we do multiple things at once because we are bored, or afraid of being bored. This brings up more not-so-great news for spiritual seekers. Bad news part two is that spiritual maturity also partly grows out of the capacity to just be bored when things are boring. Not a happy truth (at least at first) but there it is. To add even more insult, our brains are wired in a way that makes it easier to get distracted than to pay attention to one thing. Srini Pillay, an assistant clinical professor at Harvard Medical School, put it this way: Because the part of our brain that is devoted to paying attention is connected to our emotional center, any strong emotion can make us just want to, oh, I don't know, pencil in an eyebrow at a stop light. In the meantime our lives are passing us by and death is coming closer.

Enter the miracle problem solver. Outside of serious drugs with nightmare-inducing side effects, simple mindfulness in the form of meditation has an inherent power to allow for our changing from multitasker extraordinaire to a unitasking happy camper. For proof, please use your own experience. You will find that— if you stick with it—meditation can reset your distraction buttons, partly by demonstrating that you won't die from boredom and partly because it pretty much forces you to do one thing at a time—that is, sit. At first, the only positive result that most of us experience from meditation is a lessening of stress. This is usually followed by shock at how much stress we have internalized into our body-minds. Our incessantly chattering brains clearly show each of us our personal karmic patterns of distraction. It is never pretty, although, if you are like me, it can be pretty funny. For some of us, it's worry. For others, an obsession with sex. Sometimes it's creative thinking. Whatever we find, we get a chance, through mindfulness, to simply observe what is right in front of us—our own thoughts—in a safe place on a meditation cushion.

When I finally slowed down enough to genuinely watch my own thoughts, to say I was shocked is an understatement at best. I've already talked about the multitude of simultaneous ticker-tape parades. When I really watched, I saw that one ticker tape consisted of my main line of thinking. Usually this took a form of problem solving. The second tape was typically some type of to-do list that grew out of the first line. So if I was thinking about when I needed to pick my daughter up from school, behind that would be a note-taker saying, "Find a babysitter with a driver's license." Behind that, I'm not proud to say, the third ticker tape, when it wasn't humming a song, was a schoolteacher-like voice reminding me to count my breaths. Part of why it took a long time to let go of multiple tracks of thinking was that I actually got a lot of work done on the cushion. In one retreat I wrote an entire screenplay. (It was terrible but made the retreat fly by.) On the other hand, my lazy spiritual effort was leading nowhere when it came to advancing toward a life where my habit to go, go, go was transformed to one of calm unitasking.

I was a mess and I knew it. I wanted to stop the multitracks, but they were so habituated that I was terrified that I'd never be free of them. Honestly, if it had occurred to me to text while driving and putting on makeup at a stoplight, I probably would have done it because, hey, time saved is money earned.

My teacher gave me two pieces of advice. The first was to stop multitasking at work. It took a slew of post-it note reminders and at least a dozen visits from colleagues asking if I was sick, but I pulled off doing one thing at a time in about a month and a half. I could just sit and read my email. I could just answer the phone. Even after that amount of time, I felt like I was cheating somehow, doing only one thing.

Then he gave me this instruction: Whenever I caught myself being distracted by more than one thing, I should simply refocus on my bright moon mind, wherever I was, and whatever I was doing. This gesture became a reset button that I still use to this day. In the meantime it is humbling to admit that unitasking is way more interesting than I ever imagined. It allows for multiple senses to join in one particular experience. The world becomes wondrous. And each thing becomes a particular pleasure. My real breakthrough came with eating without reading. Foods have all kinds of subtle tastes under and around their primary flavors. Who knew?

Apparently this Zen practice of refocusing has shown up in more and more business settings, without the bright moon mind part. Dr. Pillay, for one, suggests to his clients that the counterpoint to a distracted mind is "visualizing a reset device in your brain and saying: 'I need to press the reset button and get back on track.'" In this way our minds go back to the task at hand. Back to the one track. Or to no track at all. Pillay says it this strongly: "You are rewiring your brain."

The only reason that young woman in Eugene didn't end up in a car crash was because the man behind her, and the drivers behind him, were paying enough attention to what they were doing to protect her. The next time this might not be so. I cringe to think that I was her, years ago, and thank Buddha that help has been as near as my little meditation cushion, the one with the moon waiting for me to join it.

LOVING WHAT IS

This morning I woke up with bronchitis. If I don't stop doing everything and rest, the slide into pneumonia is slippery and fast. It turns out that living in inner city Detroit for several years back in the 1990s wrecked my lungs. First I learned how to be asthmatic. Then I took up a penchant for pneumonia. As a result I get to have a personal retreat week each winter—the week when a lingering cold downshifts in a matter of days into finding myself in the office of a doctor telling me that I should be heading into a hospital. I always negotiate my way out—promising not to move and to take baths and showers and all the drugs he or she wants to throw at me.

From that moment on, everything that has been planned for the next few weeks gets erased. Today that means no teeth cleaning appointment this afternoon. No walk with my daughter tomorrow or next week. No cookie baking for Friday's noontime meditation with my Occupy Eugene friends. No grocery shopping. No coffee at the Metropol with a friend. No Beau this weekend. Next week: repeat. The week after that repeat again. The week after that: just don't think about it.

I get out the old flannel pajamas, the gray pair with dog pictures surrounded by tea stains, and put them on. For additional warmth I hunt down my old gray wool cap, the one I've worn at every winter retreat for decades. I put that on as well.

Then I remember the dog. I need to ask Jeffrey if he'll walk him for me. I'm sure he'll say yes, but just thinking about it reminds me how vulnerable I am. It turns out I'm not an island after all. I need help. The willingness to feel vulnerable does not come easily. I'm already cranky about the missed walk, cookies, and coffee date. I'm irked. Uncomfortable.

Staying with the feeling, I watch it expand into an overriding feeling of uneasiness. This bronchitis could kill me; a hundred years ago it would have. Instead of running away from the feeling, I'm determined to stay put. It's not like I have anything better to do, after all. Surprisingly, after about twenty minutes (only twenty minutes!) it grows into a feeling of gratitude—for this moment, for the pajamas, for a roof over my head, for throat lozenges, for a phone I can have next to me, for Jeffrey. The gratitude kicks in even as the bronchitis kicks in harder. I spend the rest of the week looking out my bedroom window at the teeny garden, sipping lemon ginger tea. I notice that the gray-blue Buddha standing in front of the bamboo fence doesn't budge, and he is way more vulnerable than me. He's completely covered in frost, and it is supposed to rain later—icy rain. As mornings shift into afternoons and then evenings, I feel luckier and luckier somehow. Whole days come and go, with nothing to show for them except the passing of time and an award-winning bed head.

I was raised to be special. My mother only stopped encouraging me to run for president when Obama was elected. I guess she figured he would do. I was also raised to be completely independent—to make my own money, buy my own house, raise my kids without any help from extended family. None of these laudable intentions led to the happiness I feel sitting in bed with three layers of flannel on and a small pharmacy of drugs within reach. I'm not special. And I can't go it alone. None of us can. Eventually reality kicks each of us in the ass and tells us that we need to learn how to admit to the truth of our vulnerable not-so-special lives if we ever want to be happy, let alone sane.

Sociologists like Brene Brown have been telling us this for years: that okayness, which she defines as a strong sense of self combined with a feeling of connection to the world, comes from having the courage to be exactly what we are—imperfect and vulnerable. This includes having the guts to just be sick when we have other things we want to do. It includes asking for help with our pets or a willingness to say, "I love you" first. We each have our own list.

My own experience is that what emerges out of this place of owned imperfection and vulnerability is (brace for it) love—love as compassion, as empathy, as aliveness. Love as authenticity. Instead of wanting to make the uncertain certain, we learn to love the uncertainty and with it, all of our imperfections. There is a hilarious story that shows up somewhere in the collection of Zen Buddhist koans where a student learns about this from his teacher. He asks, "Do Zen Masters fart?" The teacher's response? He farts a big, noisy horn-blow of a fart. Shocking behavior for a spiritual teacher. And a perfect response. He wasn't about to let the student paint him as anything he wasn't. Humans fart. We make mistakes. We get to feel vulnerable. We get sick.

Shakyamuni Buddha talked about this often. Over and over he

taught his disciples that the human condition is made up of gain *and* loss, fame *and* disrepute, praise *and* blame, pleasure *and* pain. We lose our way spiritually when we ignore, cling, or run from anything: "Here monks, the uninstructed worldling . . . with the change and alteration of form, his consciousness becomes preoccupied with the change . . . he is frightened, distressed, and anxious, and through clinging he becomes agitated."[9]

When we acknowledge these aspects of our lives instead of running away, our mindfulness grows along with our okayness. Why? Because we aren't trying to protect ourselves from anything. We live barrier free, if you will. In this openness, our eyes, ears, noses, and bodies can do their work. We discover that wherever we are we live in a jaw-droppingly beautiful world, just as it is. In this place of "just this," our minds become clear mirrors. When red comes, red is reflected. Pure red. When white comes, pure white. Anything that happens to us simply becomes a component of the sweet dance of life we call ours. Precious. This includes pajama days with rolls of toilet paper sitting next to our heads.

Retreat Meals

I learned how to cook from a French chef living at the Zen Buddhist Temple in Toronto. A day into a winter retreat I was sent to the kitchen to be his noble assistant. Apparently his regular helper had disappeared. The eyebrow-to-eyebrow frown that acknowledged my appearance looked like the photos and drawings of Zen masters you see in old sutra books, the ones where their eyebrows join together in a perfect V. I can't say I blamed him. At the time I was notoriously unmindful, clumsy, and full of smart-ass. I was just beginning to learn the protocol for everything from how to enter a meditation hall to how to meditate without falling asleep or at least without snoring.

Monsieur le chef nodded at me, all six-foot-something of shoulders and muscle, and pointed at a huge box of onions.

"Chop those."

I need to mention here that I was raised by a woman who spent little time cooking. My siblings and I were raised on the first iterations of Hamburger Helper, starting when it first appeared on grocery shelves. I, for one, loved it. One-pot meals made cleaning the kitchen a fast exercise. It almost never edged into television or homework time. When frozen TV dinners—bless you, Swanson—showed up, they became our formal dinners, treats we were given on Thursdays when my parents headed to the country club for their weekly join-up with friends.

When I appeared in Toronto in my late thirties, I didn't really know how to cook eggs, let alone stir-fry a meal or cook rice. I had only recently discovered that potatoes grow under the ground. I definitely didn't have a clue about chopping onions.

What I did have was a fearlessness about trying new things and the energy of six dharma students rolled into one female body. I grabbed a knife and started chopping away. He lasted all of three minutes before he shouted, "Stop!" Or maybe it was "Merde!" I'm pretty sure it was "Merde!" This in a silent retreat. Tsk.

By then onion pieces had sprayed across the counter and into the sink, several feet away. Pieces were on the ground and in the kitchen doorway. A few were under my left foot. I don't remember moving my foot at all. A Zen miracle? He slowly, frowningly— think large V—taught me how to correctly chop onions. First, it is important to make sure the knife is sharp. Mine wasn't even close. He showed me how to scrape it along a thin, slightly corrugated metal rod. By this point I was weeping profusely from the mashed onions all around us, so it was a little hard to see what he was demonstrating. Then he showed me how to peel an onion. Oops again. From there he painstakingly showed me how to first slice an onion in half lengthwise, then into quarters, then into eighths until I could chop the whole thing into tiny, perfect little squares.

"Pay attention. You must pay attention."

In my imagination he smiled at that point.

It took the entire retreat to chop all the onions in the box and another three years to master correctly chopping onions and other vegetables into neat little squares. Here's a secret I discovered along the way: Whenever I want to know how I'm doing, vis a vis mindfulness, including today, all I have to do is look at an onion I've chopped up. The same is true for all fruits and vegetables. When the pieces are even and neat and piled somewhere carefully, mindfulness fills the air. When the pile is messy and/or pieces are uneven and/or I have pieces of whatever it is around my feet, I've been lost in the land of planning or worrying. A simple, foolproof indicator, this. I've learned to use the odd-sided little vegetable pieces as a reminder to amp up energywise, until I can feel mindfulness take over. Life is too short to waste. Time to be awake to what is actually going on.

A side bonus that has come from cooking hundreds of retreat meals since then is that I've become quite the chef. Not only do I love cooking everything from stews to stir fries from scratch, but retreatants actually enjoy the food. Back in the Toronto days, one of the other "sous chefs" said to me that when we put our hearts into our cooking, the people eating the food will be filled not just with the food but with our love as well. I recall looking at him like he was nuts and seriously thinking that it might be a good time to run away from the loony bin of a Zen kitchen. Thank goodness I didn't because, years later, I have to say he was right.

A perfect retreat meal:

1. Barley tea: Asian grocery stores carry this inexpensive tea. Buy it in bulk. For a pot, put a handful of barley into a teapot that holds at least 4 cups of liquid. Add fully boiling water. (No cheating here. The hotter the water the better the tea.) Fill the teapot and let it steep for the duration of the retreat meal. Covering the pot with a thick cloth like a tea towel will keep the water hot for quite a while. As soon as the main meal is finished, pour the tea into teacups or emptied bowls, using a tea strainer to keep the barley behind in the teapot. Sip slowly if there is time. Barley tea is wonderfully calming, has no caffeine, and must have significant health benefits, given its nutty, fresh taste.

2. Brown rice: Also can be purchased in bulk. Also inexpensive. Put 1½ cups of rinsed rice (to clean away any dirt, dead bugs, undefinable grit) into a heavy pot. Add 3 cups of water. Bring to a boil, and then cover the pot and cook on low until the rice is the consistency you want. Depending on the pot and the stove you are using, this can take anywhere from 10 minutes upward. The cooking rice needs to be periodically checked to make sure it doesn't burn along the way. (It is okay to add more water if you need to.) I have yet to find a way to reuse burned rice for anything except chicken feed, and even

then I've had chickens look at me like I'm stupid and just walk away from the offering.

3. Tofu and vegetables in spicy peanut sauce. Chop up at least 1 large peeled onion, and mince at least 2 cloves of peeled garlic and ½ inch of fresh peeled ginger. Set aside. Then chop up a head of broccoli or a big bunch of kale or collards (or all three—you decide) into 2-inch pieces. Set aside. Chop up a 14-ounce block of firm tofu into small squares. An inch or slightly less is nice. Set this aside as well.

In a medium-sized mixing bowl, stir these together: ¼ cup soy sauce; ¼ cup molasses; ½ to 1 cup of chunky peanut butter, depending on taste and budget; at least 1 teaspoon of hot sauce. (I like to use a lot more, but then I enjoy food that blisters the inside of my mouth.) You can also add unsalted roasted or raw peanuts, at least a handful, if you like. Keep adding soy sauce, molasses, and hot sauce to the mixture until the combination makes your heart sing. You'll know when that is. In a big frying pan, preferably an old iron skillet that looks like it belongs in Montana in 1850, heat up enough oil to cover the bottom of the pan. The only oil I've found that doesn't work is olive oil. When in doubt, canola oil and generic vegetable oil work and are cheap.

As soon as the oil starts to spit a little, which happens almost as soon as the heat is turned on to medium high, stir-fry the onions, garlic, and ginger for a minute or so, or until the onions are translucent. Add the tofu and green vegetables. Stir-fry until the vegetable colors look slightly brighter. Then add the sauce concoction and turn the heat down to simmer. If the sauce is too thick, you can add a little water slowly or even some vegetable bouillon until the dish is the consistency you want.

Once the rice is cooked and the sauced-up tofu and vegetables are hot enough to burn your mouth, the meal is read to eat. It should serve four to six people, depending on how hungry everyone is.

For side dishes, kimchee (a pickled cabbage that is spicy due to being mixed with red hot chilis and left alone for at least two days), more peanuts, raw vegetable sticks, and apple slices are all delicious. For a sweet, almond cookies and fresh fruit like sliced pineapple or kiwi can make this an unforgettable meal. There won't be any leftovers, regardless of how neatly the vegetable pieces have been cut.

2: Investigation of Phenomena

Gradually, the mind learns through meditation to be content merely within itself; the mental processes are progressively calmed, and the student achieves absorption—pure mental concentration. Eventually, the concentrated power created through this absorption is turned toward an investigation of himself, his world, and the relationship between the two. This investigation develops wisdom, which teaches him about the processes of life and leads him to discover the true nature of himself and, indeed, of all things. —ZEN MASTER CHINUL[1]

WHERE DID I COME FROM?

WHEN I WAS in graduate school, I once went to a party where, after no small amount of drinking, the host announced that his date could sing the alphabet backwards. After much cajoling, she sang for us. We loved it, and her. When she was done, one of the other grad students stood up and announced that he could recite Othello front to back. We knew him too well to ask him to demonstrate. It turned out that everyone there could recite at least one book or long poem. *Howl* for example. We ended up going around in a circle, naming our titles. When it was my turn, I announced that I had memorized *Where Did I Come From?* by Peter Mayle. You may be familiar with it: "This book is all about you. We wrote it because we thought you'd like to know exactly where you came from, and how it all happened. And we know (because we have children of our own) how difficult it is to tell the truth without getting red in the face and mumbling."[2]

I managed to recite the first half-dozen pages before I ran out of breath. When my friends were able to stop laughing—with me, not at me—we ended up seriously talking about the question of where "I" comes from. In Buddhism this is an important question.

Where *do* we come from? Those of us who have been determined to follow the thread backwards typically end up dead-ended somewhere in the land of physics or divine will. It becomes a scary question at this point, because there seems to be nowhere to go. This is exactly the point where Buddha's admonition to pay attention becomes critically important. Turning to sutras can also trigger some understanding here. The Diamond Sutra, for example, tells us that everything is impermanent and empty. There is no room for an I. This is a teaching completely consistent with Buddha's teaching that what we call I is only a collection of forms, feelings, perceptions, impulses, and consciousness. Okay. Assuming that Buddha is correct, where does I start?

One powerful method for getting to where we can literally see for ourselves is to be curious. Why? Because wide-open curiosity can take us right through the dead space between teachings and our own experience into a genuine understanding (because we can actually "see" it) of where our I starts.

If you have never tried paying this kind of attention to your own life, it helps to have a teacher, someone gifted in the art of curiosity. My vote goes to Sherlock Holmes. This iconic detective spent some twenty-three years, as documented in four novels and over fifty short stories, teaching his readers the fine art of investigation of phenomena in a way that is both understandable and wildly entertaining. Setting aside his arrogance and cocaine use, Holmes is a master of this form of investigation. When he first meets his noble assistant, Dr. Watson, he is able to tell Watson all sorts of things about how he spends his days—just by looking at his shoes. From that moment, Watson becomes a surrogate for you and me. We get to see how our level of curious attention compares to Holmes's experiences with the crimes they (mostly) solve. At one point, Holmes asks Watson the simple question of how many steps there are up to Holmes's door. Watson, who has been walking up and down the stairs on a daily basis, can't answer. Holmes's reaction? We get a lecture on the huge difference between noticing something and really paying attention to it. There is a difference between seeing something and genuinely observing it. (There are seventeen stairs.)

When we take on this task of being deeply curious, we will notice that the attention itself takes on particular characteristics. First, it becomes impersonal. In Holmes's case, even when beautiful young women and children are involved in a crime, Holmes is interested more in the structure of the crime itself. For us, emotions come and go with less and less fire in them, allowing us to see patterns and make connections that we never noticed before. Second, this curious attention is impartial. In Holmes's cases, every clue gets the same level of attention. In the same way, we start to see how we aren't the center of anyone's universe, including our own. This makes it easier and easier to follow threads of habits back to their beginnings. We discover habits we never knew we had. I had no idea how much time I spend straightening our pictures, blinds, cushions, and lap blankets every day. Hmmmmmm. Third, this form of investigation is patient. A crime will be solved when it is solved. Likewise, we'll be able to see our conditioned knots of emotions and habits when we do, and not a minute sooner. Fourth, this kind of attention is fearless. Holmes never knows where clues will lead him.

A good teacher shows us that nothing is too small to observe. As we shift from seeing to observing, it becomes more and more apparent that everything that happens to us can be traced back to a moment, a word, a gesture—for better or worse. When I started to pay attention to my marriage instead of keeping my head buried under as many pillows as were in the house, I was suddenly able to pinpoint the exact day when the great unraveling began. It was a fall day when my husband went to school an hour early and came home late. Months later, when I finally had the courage to bring up his new commuting pattern, my husband openly admitted to the affair that triggered our parting ways. While it was painful at the time, my curious observing probably saved both of us years of unquiet, not to mention a mortally wounded marriage. In the same way, I remember the moment when I realized that my friend Jeffrey was more than a friend. We were at the library, and he was turning an old Zen koan into a children's story at a summer camp program. I saw him watching me even as he was telling the kids the story. And I realized that I was watching him back just as intently. This ending is happier.

Curious attention is honest. It doesn't cloud. It just points. We find out what makes I and how everything in our life feeds this identity in one way or another. We also see what helps us to let go of our grip on this me, given that it isn't going to last all that long anyway. Life is short, after all.

There is a last gift that comes from such curiosity. If we follow the good detective's footsteps, the world that seemed to close up tightly with our grade school teacher's instruction to color inside the lines bursts forth, literally. This is the world where improbable things happen all the time, where we watch the miracle of birth and death unfold before our very eyes every day. In this world, we laugh completely and we cry completely, and we can catch leaves as they fall from trees because we know how to pay attention. This world nurtures us, grass blade by grass blade, and shows us—by giving us immeasurable things we can investigate—where we come from.

SEEING THROUGH THE LENS AFFECTIONATELY KNOWN AS ME

When my son was a baby, I made him a thick quilt out of six-inch cotton squares that had faces of children and baby animals on them. He loved the quilt enough to want to take it to: preschool, grandmom's, the doctor's, the dentist's, the grocery store, and the playground. We called it his nung-nung. When he started big-kid school in first grade, he had a terrible time giving up nung-nung, even though it was so stained and patched that his teacher insisted we leave it at home. Somewhere around the middle of second grade, he finally lost interest in the quilt, even when he was sick. I knew it was time to put it away.

Years later my daughter spotted it in one of our old boxes and asked if she could use it. At five she seemed a little old for a nung-nung. I patched it up anyway. She kept it in sight all the way through grade school. It was in her closet during high school. After that we both lost track of it until a few years ago when it showed up in one of our many moves. These days it keeps my grandson company, stains and all.

I've always been surprised by how many people have stories about their own nung-nungs. My college boyfriend shocked a hand-ful of us on a date night when he waxed poetic about his favorite childhood blanket. It was satin. When he was done describing it and how he always had it "on him"—this in the days before tat-toos—he proceeded to pull his wallet out of his pants pocket and open it up to show us all a scrap of cloth—the last piece of his beloved blanket.

We all have nung-nungs. Actually we all share the mother of all nung-nungs which I'll summarize as the great comforter com-monly known as me. And oh how we cling. We want the world to be the way we want it to be. It needs to be easy for *me* to live this life. *My* family deserves to have an easy, fulfilling, wealth-inducing, gift-filled life because, well, we're good people, after all.

Of all the obvious problems that come with this nung-nung, starting with the fact that life is really hard for everyone, the queen of all problems is this one: It can completely block spiritual growth. We may manage to conjure up all kinds of bliss and even some clarity while we live in the land of me, but a fully awakened life? No chance. The possibility of being of service to the world as it is, or what Zen Buddhism calls the bodhisattva life, isn't going to take, either. Not until we give up the blanket.

Knowing this doesn't make letting go of me any easier. I speak from hard-won experience here. Having said this, it turns out that meditation, mindfulness, and doing our best to keep an open, curious mind have their own ways of magically chipping away at me. One of the first signs that the practices are having an impact is our seeing how completely driven we are by our identities. For those of us who have the courage to look, what we'll see is a long parade of acts of greed, anger, and delusion, all geared at protecting this identity. Just take thoughtlessness, as one example. We neglect to take out the trash because we're too busy with matters of consequence, leaving it for someone else, or for the next week. As for my own parade, this week I had to take the dog to the vet because I completely ignored how much he was scratching his left ear. Now it's infected. Last week I teased my granddaughter about a cooking class she was taking over the summer. She was on her second round of being grounded only one week into high school. "Well," I said, "You'll be able to cook good food for everyone in the mission when you're homeless." I was thoughtless and unkind, protecting the me who didn't want to be embarrassed by a granddaughter making her own way in the world. This after a quarter century of hard spiritual practice and endless vows to be kind. May she hear my many apologies.

Fortunately the same quarter century has taught me that the me nung-nung shrinks with time. I'd hate to think of what I was like before I discovered this path. We're also helped by teachers who have the capacity to conjure up moments where we can taste what it's like to be freed from the lens of me. My root teacher, Samu Sunim, used to demand that we shout ourselves hoarse when we went into one-on-one interviews with him, particularly during long retreats. For years, fifty or sixty of us would sit in long rows facing the walls hearing roars of "Mu!" or "What is it?" If we didn't shout loudly from our bellies when it was our turn, he would roar right into our faces from about two feet away until we out-shouted him. These interviews were my first experience of no me. Eyeball to eyeball with Sunim there was just shouting. Nothing else. The first time it happened I was so overwhelmed and relieved that I wept through the next sitting. It felt like I had been given a chance to fly out of a cage I hadn't known I was in.

Unfortunately, even for longtime teachers—no matter what they say or how they act—there is always at least a scrap of our nung-nung velcroed to our minds. So we all get to keep practicing together, none of us special. And as we do, two things happen. First, we spot me sooner and sooner, sometimes catching it before we open our mouths. This grows out of an ever more skillful watchfulness. Second, more and more of our time is free of outbursts related to trying to protect ourselves. We exchange anger, greed, and delusion for more empathy, compassion, equanimity, and joy. We learn that we can't will these states into our systems but that they will grow as we let go of clinging to our timeworn notions of who and what we are.

For those of us who continue to need surrogate nung-nungs during this transition period, a spiritual guide is just the ticket. This is someone who, with his or her words or actions, can push us when we need pushing, comfort us when that could help, and give us instructions when we ask. In the Korean Buddhist lineage, the Zen monk Chinul has always played that role for me. I was introduced to him via a quote: "Do not fear the arising of thoughts: only be concerned lest your awareness of them be tardy." With these words he is doing all three things: pushing, comforting, and giving instructions. It doesn't matter that he lived in Korea in the twelfth century. What does matter is that his words can bring us back to the world as it is in a way that opens up a courage to put down the nung-nung of me again and again and again, for all of our sakes.

"Cultivate earnestly and the power of contemplation will grow; train continuously and your practice will become increasingly pure. . . . If you always remember your good fortune, you will never backslide. If you persevere in this way for a long time, naturally *samadhi* and *prajna* will become full and bright and you will see your own mind-nature; you will use compassion and wisdom like sorcery and ferry across sentient beings; you will become a great field of merit for men and gods. I urge you to exert yourselves!"[3]

EVERYBODY SUFFERS

You know how when you hear an unfamiliar sound in the middle of the night your whole body goes on alert? It's like every cell in your body is asking, "What was that?!" Your ears become as sensitive as a cat's, and your whole body-mind is completely focused until you can identify the sound. It doesn't even matter if you are wrong. The wondering doesn't go away until you name the sound.

That wondering is a taste of the great doubt that Zen teachers refer to when they encourage each of us to have great doubt, great faith, and great determination. Great doubt is where we ask, "What is this?" and stay alert enough to move through our guessing about what is going on to actually seeing, hearing, tasting, or feeling the truth of the situation we find ourselves in. When we allow ourselves to deeply question in this way, a different world

41

opens—an honest one. In this world, unexpected truths appear. One is that everybody suffers. Everybody. Knowing this makes it easy to understand why Shakyamuni Buddha spent his entire forty-five years of teaching focused on suffering and its cessation.

The first time I realized that suffering might be universal happened when I was in high school. I knew kids suffered, because I grew up in a big family surrounded by four younger siblings. We all got sick, scrapped, felt ashamed when we screwed up, and were hurt when our friends and later boyfriends and girlfriends were mean to us. Since my parents never fought in front of us, never cried, and were rarely sick, it never occurred to me that adults might also suffer, especially beautiful, rich, young adults who had the world on a string. That was my parents.

Nouveau riche doesn't even begin to describe our lifestyle. For some years, before my father lost everything in an economic downturn, we were probably one of the wealthiest families in Australia. To give you an example of the nouveau part, when we first moved to the country, my father insisted on shipping his dark green Chrysler convertible over from the United States. It was the only car of its kind in the country. Whenever we drove into Sydney, people would stop and wave, figuring that we were somebody important. And while our house wasn't huge, we had a swimming pool, a full-time gardener, personal tutors, and a massive refrigerator in the garage just for beer. We five kids attended the best boarding schools Australia had to offer.

My parents didn't throw many parties, but when they did they were doozies. My father played popular songs on the piano so people could sing along—an early version of karaoke. There was always lots of laughter, lots of singing, lots of drinking, lots of food.

One party night I was sneaking past my parent's bedroom to nab some party food for us kids when I saw one of my parents' friends sitting on their bed with tears streaming down her cheeks. She was young, beautiful, and wealthy (given the size of her wedding ring). I just stared at her, stunned, trying to register what I was seeing.

It was suffering.

She was clearly suffering from head to toe. I was too shocked, and nervous about getting caught roaming, to do anything but continue along my stealthy way. Still, her image has stayed with me all these years.

Later, as a young adult in my pre-Zen days, I worked for a gazillionaire who ran one of the biggest philanthropic foundations in the world. He was blunt, abrasive, and brilliant. Many people were put off by him in a matter of minutes. I was too fascinated to do anything but wonder what was up with this guy. As I watched him, it dawned on me—slowly—that he was also suffering. It turns out that it really is lonely at the top. You never know who you can trust. Genuine friends are rare. So is humor, for some reason. I saw a sadness in him that I'm guessing most other people missed. We became friends. He taught me how much suffering there really is, especially in the people we never expect to be having a rough go. Buddha ran into this all the time. Kings suffered. Courtesans suffered. Warriors suffered. Brahmins suffered.

For me, when this realization of suffering sank in, a couple of things happened as a result. I've seen the same unfolding in hundreds of Zen students over the years. First, we start to trust our understanding of what is happening in our lives. We are seeing things, hearing things, and understanding things more accurately. This is huge. Bhikkhu Bodhi makes a strong point about this: "The

Buddha does not demand that we *begin* our spiritual quest by placing faith in doctrines that lie beyond the range of our immediate experience. . . . He asks us to consider a few simple questions pertaining to our immediate welfare and happiness, questions that we *can* answer on the basis of our personal experience."[4] In other words, we need to fine-tune our wondering mind to where we can really see ourselves clearly. For some reason, seeing the world more clearly leads us right back to ourselves. Every time.

As an example from his own life, on one occasion Buddha was staying in a town called Uruvelakappa when its headman, Bhadraka, approached him to ask him about suffering. Buddha, agreeing to explain it, turned the question back on Bhadraka, asking how he would feel if people he knew were harmed. The headman answered that he would feel sorrow, lamentation, pain, dejection, and despair. So not only would the people themselves be suffering, but knowing of their suffering he would suffer, as well. As he looked at his own suffering he saw how it grew out of a feeling of desire—that he wanted people to be safe and healthy and happy. From the moment he woke up, this was first in his mind as he checked on his sleeping son.

When we ask ourselves what is going on in our own lives, a similar response will surface. If we aren't happy, almost always there will be some form of suffering in the way. Usually it is our own. We don't have what we want: a better car, job, house; drug-free kids. We have what we don't want: bills, a lousy job, a worse boss, no job. Sometimes we suffer because of the suffering that we see all around us. Parents know this form of suffering well. Having the courage to acknowledge this shared feeling turns out to be a step toward a genuine path of happiness. We can't help others if we don't admit that there is a need. We can't change until we own up to our own capacity to make ourselves suffer. We can't grow up until we do both.

WHERE DOES MEXICO START?

"Borders are the sediments of history, and the stuff that armchair expeditions are made of," writes Frank Bruni. "Even though, in today's Europe, national borders like these feel more internal than international, they still amount to something. They're invisible obstacles, a bit like glass ceilings, but vertical and spatial rather than horizontal and hierarchical. Neighbors on either side of a borderline are oriented toward their respective national capitals, have different holidays, read their own newspapers, even build their houses differently."[5]

My first real job as a new Ph.D. was working on the program staff of a major philanthropic foundation. I joined the community development team. Two of us, my boss and I, were given the mandate of working with nonprofit groups at the grassroots level who were doing everything they could to get better housing, schools, services, and jobs into their communities.

One of the first site visits I got to make was to Texas to visit a group trying to help immigrants coming to the United States from Mexico. The group was mostly made up of church people, as I recall. One afternoon I was taken to a hillside overlooking a skinny, filthy little river to watch people cross over. Within the first half hour we watched a couple of teenagers run down a hill from the other side, put the parcels they were carrying on their heads, and wade/swim across the river. At the other side they didn't bother to

dry off. Instead they ran up the hill and into the suburban neighborhood that backed up the berm where we were sitting.

I looked at the woman I was with. "You have got to be kidding
me."

They were the ages of my little sisters. I'd never be able to pick
them out of a crowd.

She nodded. That little almost-dried-up river was the boundary
between Mexico and the United States. At the time there were no
fences that I could see and no border patrol. Just an incredibly hot
sun and some big bushes at the top of the berm. One of the main
projects of the group I was visiting was to protect the kids coming
over from being robbed, beaten, and raped when they made it to
the top of the hill on our side. That's all. The group didn't have the
resources to offer anything more than a little physical safety.

Watching the kids, I was too shocked to do anything but stare.
That was the border we were spending millions of dollars a year to
protect? A sewer-filled puny little river? And where was the exact
border anyway? Down its middle? On its U.S. side? The Mexican
side?

Thirty years later I can still close my eyes and see the berms,
the river, and the sun. I can still see the two men crouched behind
a bush a block away from us waiting for the teens—the men who
left them alone because they saw the two of us watching them. I'm
still curious. Where does Mexico start really? My neighborhood
feels like Mexico, and I live in Oregon. The soccer players in my
park shout at each other in Spanish. When I pass other strollers I
am greeted with "Hola" as often as "Hi." I can walk to two Mexican
grocery stores. The flowers planted all around the neighborhood

oil change place are the colors of the Mexican flag. Cinco de Mayo is a major celebration. In this house we all speak Spanish, even though we're northern European mongrels.

Where does anywhere start? My experience in Texas and later, close to the border between South and North Korea, left me confused. Why do we have borders? We're all members of family tribes really, little ones, tribes that want our members to be safe, fed, housed, clothed, and loved, regardless of the name of the country we dwell in. So what's with the borders? The South Koreans I know hate being separated from their families and friends in North Korea. The Texans I met hated living with the border. Mostly, they told me, it didn't do anything but piss people off for one reason or another.

In *The Dhammapada*, one of the first collections of teachings from Shakyamuni Buddha, there is a line that says, "With our minds we make the world." That we have made borders with our minds breaks my heart. This teeny little Earth feels too ragged these days to be spending so much time and energy on manmade boundaries that ultimately can't be defended anyway. Perhaps you have noticed.

Zen Master Seung Sahn has a teaching on this that has always triggered a helpful investigating mindfulness for me. He tells a story about how one day Buddha asked his attendant, Ananda, where the bell sound was coming from when a temple bell was being rung.

Ananda was quick to respond: "The bell."

Buddha teased him a little. Oh, really? If there wasn't a stick to hit the bell, then what?

Ananda's response? "The stick! The stick!"

Buddha was on a roll. Oh yeah? Well, what if there wasn't any air? Then how could the bell sound get to us?

Ananda again: "The air."

Buddha was not going to let Ananda off the hook here, even a little. He asked him, "What about your ears?"

Ananda again, probably a nervous wreck by then: "Yes! I need an ear to hear it. So it comes from my ear."

At this point Buddha went straight to the heart of his teaching. He asked Ananda if the sound was coming from consciousness. It was. Ananda was sure of it. Well then, the Buddha replied, "What about the mind?"

"It is created by mind alone."

The investigation was complete. Buddha was silent.[6]

It turns out that when we follow the threads of our own beliefs backward we see that our minds create everything that is our world. Having a willingness to really investigate all these things our minds have created—starting with the need for borders— offers each of us an opportunity to ask ourselves if the world has been helped by our creations. And if it hasn't, this same capacity can help us figure out what "undo" can mean.

PAIN EXPLORED

It is 2:30 a.m. I am wide awake thanks to two knees that have decided to teach me about pain. Years of running and dance have caught up with me, so now, pretty much every night, these knees wake me up. Tonight I'm too tired to do more than just watch the pain and its antics, curious.

I decide to simply move into it. After all, the Buddha taught that we all experience sickness, and this includes pain. In fact in the only story I can remember where he taught someone else about pain he told him to keep doing his practice. More specifically, one of his disciples, Dighavu, in a great deal of pain, asked Buddha's advice. The reply was that he hoped the man was bearing up well. When Dighavu responded that he wasn't, the advice given was to concentrate on his spiritual practice, continue to take refuge in Buddha, dharma, and sangha, and observe the arising and ceasing of everything, including the pain.[7]

Choosing my left knee, I focus on the feeling, shape, and rhythm of the pain. At first, there is only heat. It feels solid, but then I can feel how it comes and goes in waves, keeping time with my heartbeat. I keep watching, wondering what will come next. Ah. The focal point of the pain. It is on the side of the knee. It feels like a round cut on my bone. Sharp. Time for whining. Where is that spaciousness that everyone promises?

Taking a deep breath, I keep watching. After a while there is some spaciousness and an added awareness of the right knee mirroring the left. Its most acute pain is in exactly the same spot. How interesting. I watch for a while longer, and then I get up and take two ibuprofen. Spaciousness is all well and good, but I need some sleep.

Great faith, great courage, and great questioning are what allow us to genuinely investigate the phenomena of our lives. Great faith is like a chicken who sits on her eggs until they hatch. She doesn't move. Time is irrelevant. When they hatch, they hatch. Great courage? This is having the guts to focus one hundred percent on what

49

is right in front of us, especially when we have no idea what will come next. When I can watch knee pain without distraction and with enough energy to actually feel the blood pumping through my body, I'm experiencing great courage.

Great questioning is trickier. On one level, someone who greatly questions is like a thirsty person who hasn't had anything to drink for two days. There isn't anything but the water. In the same way, there isn't anything but the question. At the same time, great questioning has to do with correctly responding to the situation we find ourselves in. What is this situation calling for? Not, what do I hope will happen, or what do I want to happen, but what is really needed? The reason why this is called great questioning is that we have to move through our own wants to see what is called for by the situation itself. At 3:30 a.m. this can mean that continuing to focus on the components of pain in the knees isn't going to do it. A lack of sleep will cause all sorts of trouble the next day. Time to get up and go for store-bought help.

These small moments of watching and deciding what is the correct thing to do matter. Why? Because they prepare us for the more difficult situations that our lives promise, the ones where we are faced with the gray areas that make those of us who want to do the right thing crazy. To report a boss who is stealing. To confront child or pet abuse. To end the relationship after decades together. It is the combined practice of great faith, courage, and questioning that gives us the strength to do what needs doing. Even when we hate it. Even when we are the only person doing it. Even when it means that we are disagreeing with our own teacher.

When I was the guiding teacher for Still Point Zen Buddhist

Temple, one of my secret guidelines for deciding that someone was ready to be ordained was that the student had to disagree with me on something that mattered deeply to him or her. The issue could surface in any number of ways, from reacting to changes in tried-and-true rituals to responding to requests for help from someone in the neighborhood known to be a chronic liar and possibly worse. Most often the "test" came up in an interview situation where we were working on koans together.

These were people who had already been practicing for several years and who had already completed at least two years of a three-year, rigorous seminary program, one that demanded full participation twenty-four hours a day, seven days a week, with only the month of August as a break.

Looking back, there was only one student I was concerned about. It was a young man who had long trained in martial arts and was used to quickly and completely obeying his instructors. He was a sangha favorite, handsome and big, twinkly-eyed and generous, with a huge Italian belly laugh that could shake the rafters.

One Sunday he showed up at the interview door as cross as a bear. As I remember it, we had been working on this koan: "Master Hyang Eom said, 'It is like a man hanging by his teeth from a branch high up in a tree. His hands and feet are tied, so his hands cannot touch the branch, and his feet cannot touch the tree. Another man standing under the tree asks him, 'Why did Bodhidharma come to China?'

"If he opens his mouth to answer, he will lose his life. If he does not answer, he evades his duty and will be killed."[8]

The question was: If you are in the tree, how do you stay alive?

My student responded correctly, with great verve. He was, in that moment, great faith, great courage, and great questioning. I responded with something like, "Perfect!"

He wasn't done. He stared into my eyes, still filled with energy, and told me that if I hadn't passed him he would have quit the seminary. It was a great honor to ordain this young man. He will always know when to get up and take two ibuprofen.

CHANNELING MORANDI

I have five paintings sitting in front of me and am marking through them so I can cut them into bookmarks. Borrowing from the fire danger language of the National Forest Service, they are a red-level frustration. I've been trying to paint a series of acrylic paintings of the same bottles for almost a year now. I got the idea from Giorgio Morandi, who painted the same sets of bottles for years. In the same room. Even so, his paintings soar. Just looking at them I can tell that he knows each bottle by heart. They probably have names. Each one is beautiful, and somehow calming. At their best, jaw dropping. I want to paint like him. So far my best efforts—the pictures painted with the almighty flow at work—are only okay. I'm missing something.

For me, Giorgio Morandi (1890–1964) is one of the great artists of the twentieth century. He lived in northern Italy, in Bologna, all his life, sharing a home with his mother and three sisters. Except for a few very brief planned trips—to get away from the summer heat, for example, or to dodge World War II bombings, Morandi never strayed from his city, or from the room he lived in, for that matter.

His deceptively simple style of painting made him an iconoclast in his time. While most of Italy was enthralled with romanticism, symbolism, and dark, rich colors that included no small amount of gold highlights, Morandi opted for simple, repeated shapes in neutral colors. They unexpectedly shout of beauty, life, and a vehement appreciation for the ordinary. When asked why he painted the same bottles and jars over and over, the artist's reply was that there was nothing more surreal and nothing more abstract and therefore nothing more interesting than reality. Amen to that.

One would think that it would be a piece of cake to paint dusty old bottles, most of them white. Not true. Give me a human face any day. Bottles are satanically simple. Mine continued to be too stilted and formal. Too jarlike, somehow. Too symmetrical. Too void of my bouncy Tigger energy.

Sometimes great faith, great courage, and great questioning means never giving up. I decide that Morandi has something to teach me and I'm going to learn it, so help me Buddha. I turn to John Daido Loori, a wonderful Zen Buddhist teacher, for help. In his book *The Zen of Creativity: Cultivating Your Artistic Self*, Loori makes the case that creativity is not only our birthright but the manifestation of our spiritual growth and as integral a part of being human as is working, talking, and thinking. I love how he writes and his own story. I copy down excerpts that feel like specific instructions. "The still point is at the heart of the creative process. In Zen, we access it through zazen. The still point is the eye of the hurricane. . . . To be still means to empty yourself from the incessant flow of thoughts and create a state of consciousness that is open and receptive."[9] He understands curiosity and how openness and receptivity feed curiosity in a way that is opposite

53

from willing something to happen. I realize that I've been willing myself to paint like Morandi. Time to stop.

Always good for ideas, my friend Jeffrey suggests that I just keep copying Morandi. He tells me that there is a long tradition of painters copying masters to get inside their heads. I'm grateful for his concern but unsure it will help. I've already copied Morandi's paintings ad nauseum. Not all of them, but more than thirty, all the ones I've been able to find so far. Every time I copy one of his paintings, I try my own again. Again, I get flat. A feeling of crowdedness. The paintings will work for wrapping paper and bookmarks, but no self respecting wall will welcome them. I do this for another few months, determined.

Then, one morning, a sudden solution while I'm meditating. I realize that I've been copying the finished product. What I need to model is the man's curiosity. Instead of painting right away, I pick up each bottle I want to paint to really study it. I feel its size, weight, and shape. I see all of its colors, some I've never noticed before. There are new curves and way more shadows than you might expect to see in a simple shape.

Then, I paint.

Hours later, I come up for air and look at what I've done.

In front of me sits a vibrant, happy painting that doesn't look much like the bottles it is supposed to represent. On the other hand, it feels just like them. I've painted something that sort of looks like Morandi but completely looks like something I would paint. It is juicy and fun. It's alive with happiness. I've been so focused on being curious that I stopped being too scared to paint and just painted. A week later the painting is on a wall where I can see it every day. And every day it makes me grin. I can still feel each bottle in my hand when I look at it. Morandi once said that what has value in painting is seeing that nothing else counts except the act of painting. That act is an act of big C curiosity manifested into form. It has taken a long and windy road to get here, but I finally understand what he means. I wonder how Morandi would react if I thanked him for being a wonderful teacher of Zen—someone who manifested mindfulness, investigation, energy, concentration, and ease every time he picked up a brush.

3: Energetic Effort

....

Strive on untiringly!
—THE BUDDHA[1]

....

WHO IS A BRAHMIN?

ONE TIME Shakyamuni Buddha decided to take a break (with five hundred monks in tow!) at a lotus pond that was near the home of a brahmin named Sonadanda. Brahmins were, and in many ways still are, the people with the highest social standing in Hindu society. Sonadanda, a famous and well-respected spiritual teacher, had heard good things about Buddha and decided to check him out: "He teaches a Dhamma that is lovely in its beginning, lovely in its middle, and lovely in its ending."[2]

When word got out that he was planning to visit Shakyamuni, five hundred other brahmins who just happened to be in the area decided to tag along to watch the two interact. A few of them were very unhappy about the situation, since Sonadanda was better born than Buddha, an esteemed scholar, and a longtime and skilled expounder of the Vedas. I won't bother to go into how handsome he was. In comparison, Shakyamuni was a punk kid.

Even so, when Sonadanda arrived at Buddha's camp he was nervous that he could lose face by asking a silly question or by not being able to answer one. Sensing this, Buddha began their conversation simply: What is a brahmin? Sonadanda responded that brahmins have specific characteristics. First, they are well-born on both the mother's and father's side. Second, they are scholars. Third, they are handsome. Fourth, they are virtuous. Fifth, they are learned and wise. Sixth, they are first or second to hold the sacrificial ladle.

Buddha wasted no time undermining the response. He asked Sonadanda this: If one of these qualities were omitted, would a person still be a brahmin?

"It is possible."

How about if one of the remaining qualities is omitted as well?

"It is possible"

Sonadanda agreed that the legacy of birth could be left out as long as a brahmin is virtuous, learned, and wise and first or second to hold a sacrificial ladle. Then he admitted that looks could also go. They played with each other for a while longer until both agreed that the minimum requirements for a person to be a brahmin were wisdom and morality. "For wisdom is purified by morality and morality is purified by wisdom."[3]

Sonadanda was so taken with Buddha's observations that he became his student then and there.

So brahmins are moral people who are wise. So far, so good. When we study the teachings we see that they have an additional quality. It is the absence of laxness—an internal energy that translates into a full body response to whatever situation they find themselves in, no matter what other people think or do. Buddha never hesitated. The old Zen masters, whose stories students learn at their teachers' feet, have the same energy. They never hesitate. Instead they fully submerge themselves in the situations presented in the stories. In so doing, they model fearlessness for the rest of us. In the same way, like Buddha, they teach us what energetic effort, or *virya*, looks like.

Brahmins have a way of appearing in our lives in moments of great crises. In my life, two brahmins stand out—my mother and a Unitarian Universalist minister named Kenneth Phifer. My mother has always had a high standard of morality, even though she grew up in the age of Mad Men and married an archetypal Mad Man sort of fellow, my father. I never saw or heard her drink, lie, gossip, or harm anyone else knowingly. She is quick to help people who need help, which meant that, growing up, we always had half as many extra kids as siblings hanging around in our house day and night. Our house was safe.

For my first term at Barnard College in New York City I lived in an old apartment building that allowed its long-term tenants to stay on and share their apartments with Barnard students. As a result I shared a space with three other students and a tiny little old lady who looked like she was a hundred years old. One of the students was a beautiful young Japanese woman. Over the course of the fall she became great friends with the old woman, confiding in her. One Friday night she came home and told the woman that she was upset and scared because she had had sex with her boyfriend. The woman's response was to scold her for being irresponsible, and when she did my Japanese housemate lost it. She threw the old woman on the floor in the hallway and started beating on her.

I was in my room studying for finals. Suddenly hearing cries for help and a gurgling sound, I opened my door, saw what was happening, and pulled my housemate off of the old woman, who looked dead. The Japanese woman ran out the door. I opened my bedroom window and yelled to some passersby to call the police; we had no phone. The police came, barely saved the old woman, and finally found my housemate running around naked in the streets, all of this in the dead of winter. I was asked to testify to everything that happened and to sign the statement that was used to commit her into Bellevue until her parents could be reached.

I didn't sleep the rest of the night and called my mother in the morning to calmly—I thought—tell her what had happened. Within hours, my mother—the one who hates being in unknown big cities and hates dealing with bureaucracies even more—took a bus from the hills of western Massachusetts into the city and went from professor to professor and bureaucrat to bureaucrat with me to get permission for me to go home early, to take my exams in Massachusetts, and to move to a new apartment. The professors were great. The bureaucrats, not so much. There weren't other rooms available in my building, and we couldn't afford better dorms. But my mother was like a dog with a bone, arguing that it was the university's job to keep its students safe on university property. Period. They needed to fix this. She wasn't unkind or angry, just clear. She became this small woman who filled offices with the energy of someone who wasn't interested in backing down. I got a new room, took the exams, and was back in the thick of university life in a matter of weeks.

The second brahmin who stands out is the Unitarian minister Ken Phifer. He was my minister when I was just starting out as a management consultant. Early on at the job, through no fault of my own, I found myself being interviewed by a reporter from Detroit's weekly business magazine about the differences in pay rates and management levels between men and women. I was honest. I told her I loved my job. Then, ever the student of statistics, my flip response to her larger question was that "the numbers tell the story." As you might guess, there were significant differences. That I loved my job became the small print to a front-page story about *moi*, complete with a large photograph.

As soon as one of my bosses got wind of the story he called me, furious, and told me he was putting me on the biggest morning talk show the following Monday, during rush hour. I was to say what he told me to say. If I didn't, I was fired. At the time I was a single mom with a five-year-old and a mortgage in a not great economy. Not knowing what to do, I went to see my minister.

Ken heard me out and asked me what I wanted to say in the interview. The truth, I told him. Reassuring me that there were other jobs out there with my name on them, he asked me when the interview was scheduled. It was sometime between 6:00 and 7:00 a.m. Ken wanted me to know that he would be up and listening to the interview, and when I told my truth he would witness it. So I did, and he did, and I wasn't fired after all. Instead I was asked to be a part of a national team whose mandate was to figure out how to help women move up through the firm's ranks faster, with more equitable pay. To this day I don't know if I would have had the courage to do the interview if it wasn't for Ken.

These, then, are today's brahmins. They notice. They understand our needs and have the wisdom to know how to help us. Sometimes this means picking us up and dusting us off when we don't have any energy to do it ourselves. Sometimes it means standing as a witness so we have the courage to do the right thing in the face of great loss. Always, always, it means bringing great energy to the situation at hand, the kind of energy that can carry each of us away from harm and toward our own true brahminism.

RACING TO THE DOOR

"Arouse your entire body with its three-hundred sixty bones and joints! And its eighty-four thousand pores of the skin." Everybody understands this English, but to understand it is one thing. To do it, to truly arouse your ENTIRE body and mind—that is quite a different matter, than simply knowing it conceptually.
—EIDO SHIMANO ROSHI[4]

One of the student practices included in the Maitreya Buddhist Seminary was racing to the door. Here's how it worked. Whenever the doorbell rang, any dharma student within hearing distance was expected to instantly drop whatever he or she was doing and run to the door as fast as possible to answer it. Because typically there were several students within doorbell hearing range, this usually became a race. It was probably pretty shocking to be a visitor greeted by a pileup of breathless barefoot adults dressed in gray robes. Our teacher never asked us to do anything he wouldn't do himself, which meant that we sometimes lost the races to him.

We were expected to respond to phone calls in the same way. Answer it on the first ring, day or night. Ditto to requests from teachers—drop everything to respond. In the early mornings, as soon as we heard the morning wake-up chant, we rushed to the meditation hall for prostrations, chanting, and a sitting, oftentimes filling the room before the wake-up call was complete. When we did 108 prostrations, or bows to the ground, before the formal sitting, the effort was so strong that the room sounded as though a dozen wrestling matches were going on at once. We threw ourselves to the ground, got up, and repeated. At the end of them, all you could hear was ragged breathing from a collection of monks and monks-to-be covered in sweat, along with occasional inadvertent giggles of happiness. Then, when we sat—wham! We really sat. Clear heads. Energized bodies. It was something.

Chores had the same instruction of energetic effort woven into them. When we were cooking, we were cooking. There wasn't anything outside of the activity of creating a nutritious and filling meal for whoever was around. When we were cleaning, as I learned the hard way through innumerable orders to go back and do it again, we were genuinely cleaning. Crevices. Cracks. The floor behind the toilet. The underside of the toilet. Sunim was teaching us how to live in a state of virya. In addition to the sheer physical effort, he was teaching us to literally lean in to whatever we were doing. Instead of cutting corners, our job was to pay full attention to the corners. One time when I was up in his bedroom/office cleaning his bathroom, he paused in his paperwork. "P'arang, you are very wasteful. Whenever I see you cleaning you use so much soap. Why is this?" He got up and walked over to the bathroom where I was, painstakingly for me, cleaning the mirror. He picked up a razor. I remember thinking, I don't remember reading anywhere about teachers slashing their students, but I backed away nonetheless. The man had a temper after all.

"I've had this razor for six years! Six years!"

I got it. Energetic effort included paying careful attention about everything involved in the action. Cleaning was as much about that as it was about the cleaning itself. Included was being mindful about the amount of detergent I was using. When I was working up a sweat as I cleaned, a teaspoon of detergent could clean his entire bathroom—I swear. In the same way, meditating is as much about the effort we put into it as it is about anything else, including form. While knowing how to sit correctly or how to breathe properly helps, if we are sitting with great energy, those things can be of any sort. And we can determine how much energy we are putting into our effort by simply watching our own minds. Not enough energy? Hello, monkey mind, in the form of planning, worrying, fantasizing, sleeping, being angry about something, anything. Enough energy? More and more spaciousness and less and less of me, with all its attendant storylines.

Because of Sunim's training, later koan practice related to energetic effort with different teachers was no problem for me. One teacher shouted at me, "The world is on fire! How do you sit in samadhi?" I writhed on the cushion, putting out embers with both hands and all fingers: pssst, psst, psst. Another teacher was so struck by my falling wildly and heavily to the ground in response to a koan question that he asked if I was in the circus or something.

By the time we reach adulthood we're all damaged goods. Maybe our parents weren't drunks or abusive or unskilled. No matter. We have still had to face getting lost, bullied, unfairly blamed, ridiculed. Our bodies don't do what we want them to do. Our kids don't. Our partners? Nope, they don't. Pets? Not always. For most of us, denial becomes our way of coping. We ignore all we can. We make up stories. We create worlds in our minds to soothe ourselves, ones where we are the stars of our own shows, shows that retreat further and further from the world as it is. The problem is that the denial never protects us from reality. Worse, it cuts happiness off at the knees.

Assuming a practice of mindfulness, energetic effort is the surprise antidote to such a life. It can cut through denial to position us to live in our sweet little shared world just as it is, happily. There is just something about this form of energy, the quick response to whatever has landed at our feet, that makes it possible for us to simply clean the sink, or respond to the email, or call our mom. We start embracing the tasks themselves, and the embracing moves out to include our own failings and frailties. We see what needs to be done to transform the failings into something more positive (or to realize they were never failings in the first place) and to better care for the frailties, whatever they are.

Every time I reread the life of Buddha, I am struck anew by the wisdom of his teachings. I swear it makes me his number-one groupie, sort of like Mel in the old HBO series *Flight of the Conchords*. I can't get enough of the man. Each time I see, more and more, how he didn't waste a word, and how literal the teachings are. Each time I am struck that his dying words to his monks were "Strive on untiringly!" His last words, and what does he say? Strive. Not walk, but strive; run for the door. Let your cleaning be a full-bodied exercise. Grab the cat before she makes it all the way out the front door. But he doesn't just say strive. He tells us to strive untiringly. To never stop. When we take his advice, we open a door to happiness in the form of an unending sense of well-being and gladness. And we discover that it is a happiness that can always be tapped. We just need to open the lock. That's why dirty toilets exist.

65

CLEANING THE HOUSE EVERY DAY

Patient forbearance is the highest sacrifice,
. . .
He's not "one gone forth" who hurts others
. . .
Not insulting, not harming, restraint according to rule,
Moderation in food, seclusion of dwelling,
Devotion to high thinking, this the Buddhas teach.[5]

We want our families to be perfect. We particularly want our partners to be perfect. We probably wouldn't mind being slightly more perfect ourselves. Since none of us are, it can be comforting to consider all the advice that can be found in the sutras on how we can uphold our end of any relationship we find ourselves swimming in. One of Shakyamuni's ancestors, Lord Buddha Vipassi, was especially generous with his advice regarding this issue. He realized that when we spend time with someone, especially when we are practicing or living with them, ours becomes an intimate relationship. Some of this comes from shared values. Some comes from simply spending time together. Some comes from doing rituals together. The day I chanted the Great Compassion Dharani at the Chicago Zen Buddhist Temple for the early morning wake-up, only to walk into a room behind the kitchen full of naked men washing themselves, taught me the truth of this teaching. That we were all completely unfazed showed me how close we had all become. We were partners.

Vipassi understood this dynamic. He instructed the monks to

forbear any unkindnesses aimed in their direction and to give up not only insulting but any thoughts of harming another person. They needed to show restraint with each other in all of their actions.

These are not hard instructions. They make sense. We can see how helpful the behaviors would be to all of our partnerships. Yet, without some energy behind our intentions, it's easy to wallow in righteousness at someone else's unskillfulness, to make mental lists of all the ways we've been wronged by those closest to us, to constantly monitor the shortcomings of others. If we are on any genuinely spiritual path we already know that we would prefer a brain that doesn't wallow in such dreck. With energetic effort behind an intention to stop these behaviors, it turns out that we can stay above board, focusing instead on forbearance, kindness, and moderation. The trick is not to aim for overnight success but to focus on cleaning the houses of our minds every day, day by day. Sometimes this will mean telling ourselves to "just let go" over and over when someone in our family has just given us unasked-for and/or unskillful advice. Let go, let go, let go. It may mean looking away when we see for the millionth time that our housemate has left her still-damp used teabag on the table in front of the couch, leaving a telltale white stain. We let go some more. If our practice is strong, we clean up the stain. We do what we have to do to keep our righteousness to ourselves—walk, run, go to the gym, whine in a journal. (I am not talking here about behaviors that physically or psychologically harm another person; with that kind of abuse my advice is one word: leave.)

We clean the mind house every day. Forever. Why? Because once we start paying attention to the consequences of our own lack of restraint we see that the strength of our relationships depends on it. We also experience the sheer pleasure that comes from being in a relationship where the assumption is that even though we aren't perfect, we are each doing our best and will get more and more skillful at holding up our end. Mistakes will be just that: mistakes. No need for doghouse time.

Five years ago I was sidelined by acute plantar fasciitis. I had been working long hours for a wonderful nursery just outside of Seattle. We were on our feet on concrete every day, often lugging around things like pots and compost that were half of our body weight. After a few months I couldn't walk after work without grimacing. By the fall, burning pains shot straight up my legs from feet that felt like they were resting on burning coals. My days consisted of getting up, going to work, coming home, and going to bed. That was it. When I finally went to see a doctor, she told me that I had to stay off my feet for a month. So I quit the job and did. My feet healed, praise Buddha and a dozen acupuncture visits, leaving only vestigial knee tendon pain to remind me that things can always get worse.

Except for walking the dog on short park tours every morning and visits to the acupuncturist, I stayed on a couch for a full thirty days. It wasn't fun, but I did it. At the end of the period, I looked around and noticed that the little apartment I lived in was filthy. Every surface was covered with dust. The bathroom was growing unrecognizable plants. I could write off some of the grime to rain in the northwest, but the truth is, the only cleaning I had done for ages was a weekly wash of sheets, clothes, and towels. End result:

filth. I felt like the fool in an old Zen story, where he sees a three-story house that he really admires and asks a carpenter if he can build the same thing for him, only without the first two stories. The carpenter tries to explain that you can't have a three-story house without the first two stories, but his words fall on deaf ears; he's talking to a fool, after all.

I was doing the same thing. I wanted the clean house without doing the cleaning. Likewise, we want perfect relationships without doing the work, without listening to Vipassi's advice. Happily I was bored enough, and better enough, to throw great energy into the cleaning of that place. I cleaned until we both sparkled and never looked back. I still clean the bathroom the same way. And I still vow to put that energy into all of my relationships. Honestly, until you've stayed up with a partner, holding her while she vomits into the toilet, knowing that this will probably lead you to follow suit some day soon, you may never know the great happiness that comes from throwing yourself into that moment of compassion and loving-kindness.

Friends who run marathons tell me that running is its own reward. Until I ran myself, I didn't believe them. I wanted to, but I just didn't. It seemed like way too much effort. But they were right. Energetic effort is its own reward, whether it comes in the form of running, cleaning, holding someone's hair out of her face, or just keeping our mouth shut even though we have the perfect comeback on the tip of our tongue. When we welcome virya into our houses every day, without ducking or making excuses, we discover its magic.

Please don't believe me; try energetic effort for yourself.

Nonstop Hundred-Foot Poles

A little over a thousand years ago an eminent young Zen master named Sekiso threw a Zen question out into the universe that those of us who love to be caught up short by Zen koans have been wrestling with ever since. His question was this: How will you step forward from the top of a hundred-foot pole?

Picture it. You are crunched into a little ball on the top of this huge pole. Someone spots you and shouts, "Hey, what are you going to do now?" If you are anything like me, your initial response will be blankness, the blankness that happens just before thinking in all its forms kicks in. This brief moment is a taste of emptiness—a state where we are wide awake but there isn't anything filling up our mind space. In this place we have 360 degrees of freedom. There is nothing to see or hear or taste or smell or think, and there is nobody to do any of these things. "Not a speck of cloud in the spacious sky" is a more poetic rendering of this nada known as emptiness. For that moment the problem of the pole is gone. Worries are gone. Our always-kvetching brains are quiet. The word *yummy* comes to mind.

Unfortunately this emptiness all by itself isn't doing much good for the world we live in or for ourselves. It's time to jump. Anyone who has wrestled with Sekiso's question for a while ultimately realizes that as long as we are breathing, every situation of our lives is its own hundred-foot pole. Some poles are easy, the poles that put us in front of a favorite educational program, an obedient three-year-old, a sleeping pet. Mostly, though, our poles aren't so great. At least half of life is filled with sorrows—from debts we can't keep up with to news that it is cancer after all. Two things help us have the courage to jump right into these predicaments. The first is that taste of emptiness, however small. It promises that behind all the large and small waves coming our way is a deep and abiding stillness where we can always rest. The second thing that helps is virya, the energy that gives us the courage to just plain leap off the pole, time and time again.

Amazingly, the correct response called for by the situation is always available to us. My Zen grandfather, Zen Master Seung Sahn, used to teach that every situation calls for three types of understanding: understanding the situation we are in, understanding our function in that situation, and understanding what the correct response is. Once we figure out the first two, the third piece just pops. I'm talking nanoseconds here. We can see this play out everywhere. For example, less than a week ago I watched a cashier at the grocery store early on a Monday morning reach across her counter to grab a man's hand and squeeze it. On the surface their interaction didn't call for that. I've seen her lots of times, and she's never squeezed my hand or anybody else's. He didn't appear to be anyone she knew, given their exchanges when she first started ringing him up. Too curious to let the situation pass, when it was my turn at the counter I asked her if he was okay. She told me she saw him every week. He never talked or looked at her until today, when he told her that he's been unemployed for over two years and is really afraid that he's seen his last job. She jumped off her pole to comfort him. Not a big gesture—simple empathy—but he walked away with a much lighter step and with shoulders that weren't curled up around his ears.

Our situations and functions can shift dramatically moment to moment. In any twenty-four-hour period I can find myself shifting from dharma teacher to dog owner to mother to neighbor to grandmom to partner and back again in a matter of moments. This morning I was on the telephone talking someone through a particular Buddhist teaching when the doorbell rang. I said goodbye and opened the door to my four-year-old neighbor. He wanted to know if I wanted to trade some eggs for some cookies. He had the eggs. Boom. I went from dharma teacher to neighbor in the two steps it took to walk to the door. Then the leap off the pole: Yes! Yes to the egg–cookie trade. Yes to catching up with one of the world's great kids. Yes to all of it.

Four years ago I spent six months living in the celebrated Pearl District in Portland, Oregon. I had given up a job in Eugene for the good life—a metrocool apartment complete with its own espresso machine and an apartment mate who was a fellow Zen practitioner. One Saturday night, out of the blue, we had one of those things-will-never-be-the-same arguments. I suddenly realized that I had made a serious mistake moving to the city. So my pole was this: I was living in the wrong place but had no other obvious place to live and little chance of finding a new job somewhere else, given an economy in free fall. At first I defaulted to a tried-and-true response: I crawled into my bed, pulled the covers over my head, and tried not to suck my thumb. After a half hour or so, a wiser part of me said, "This isn't helping. You need to think clearly."

This is where virya stepped up to the plate. Leaning into the intensity of the situation, I used my upsetness as energy. I got up, got dressed, and headed out into the neighborhood for some fresh air and space, Bodhi the Dog in tow. Two blocks later we plunked ourselves down on a brick ledge that edges an old armory. I could see a basketball game on the huge television screens in the bar across the street. Looking up, there were stars. Within minutes two young men in tuxedos sat down beside us. They told me they were groomsmen for a wedding inside the armory. A few minutes later a young couple stopped to admire Bodhi, and they plunked down as well. The groomsmen regaled us with stories of all the things that had gone wrong with the wedding so far. It sounded like just about anything that could go wrong had. A minister from the wrong faith. Flowers that made everyone sneeze. Both the bride and groom having serious second thoughts before the ceremony. The five of us laughed until we were hoarse.

Suddenly one of the groomsmen turned to me and asked what I was doing there. I said I could use some feedback and told them my story. All four had the same advice: "Time to go." They were adamant. I'd find a place to live and some form of income. They suggested places to look for apartments, gave me names of friends who worked in bakeries, since that was the kind of work I wanted. They gave me cards. Right then I knew I would head back to Eugene and do what it took to make a life there, come what may. The groomsmen insisted on walking us home, shocking the imperturbable doorman with their deep flourishes as they bowed goodbye. I felt like I had dropped into the land of beautiful young bodhisattvas—the kind who are quietly and (mostly) secretly taking care of the rest of us while we find our way home. Without virya I would have missed them completely.

GOOD FRIENDS

The Buddha often spoke of the importance of good friends. The most famous moment was when his longtime attendant and cousin, Ananda, asked him if good friends are important. Yes was the reply.

Just before he died, Buddha reiterated the importance of friendship, offering specific instructions to his followers. He was comforting the people who were already mourning the loss of him, reminding them of the behaviors that would lead to their happiness: "I will tell you another seven things conducive to welfare . . . . . As long as monks do not rejoice, delight and become absorbed in works . . . in chattering, . . . in sleeping, . . . in company, . . . in evil desires, . . . in mixing and associating with evil friends, . . . they may be expected to prosper and not decline."[6]

It turns out that our behaviors usually shift significantly when we seriously take up the spiritual path. We tend to become quieter and enjoy quieter pastimes. Activities that used to draw us to them like sirens lose their pull. Staying up late to practice "Time After Time" for the next karaoke party just isn't worth the effort. Better to sleep so we can be awake for our morning meditation or prayer. We seem to grow a sixth sense that warns us to sidestep potentially dangerous situations we used to dive into—the dope smoking days, the beer parties, the hunt for multiple sexual partners. We lose our tendencies to lie, exaggerate, need to be noticed. We aren't as tempted by entertainment. We're willing to stay home with what is right in front of us.

One result of these changes in behavior? We lose old friends.

Nobody seems to talk about this or how much it can hurt, especially when we lose a best friend. Not through death, although that is killer heartbreak, but by the simple withdrawal of their friendship. We've changed. He or she moves on. Without us.

As I write this I am watching one of my dharma brothers wrestle with the loss of his best friend, a compadre who has seen him through marriage, divorce, sickness, and health. Suddenly though, what they have in common doesn't even come close to what they don't. And it hurts. When my brother tells me about it he has tears in his eyes.

Anyone who has lost a best friend knows that it can hurt as much as losing a romantic relationship. This is someone who has known us intimately—our hopes, dreams, disappointments, and heartbreaks. She's rubbed our back while we've puked out the last margarita we'll ever drink so-help-us-Buddha. He's walked through miles—literally—of neighborhoods downtown looking for your car with you—the one you forgot you loaned to your cousin for the day. When you both see it in the driveway after a day of searching, you just look at each other and laugh.

I tell my dharma brother that I understand his sadness, that I grieved for a year when one of my best friends and I parted ways after more than thirty years of girlfriending. It was time, but that didn't matter. I still wept for the lost phone calls, the day trips, the shared sense of the world's absurdity. We had been friends from the years when we were both struggling to make our first house payments, in our early twenties. Barbara witnessed my marriage to my daughter's father. I performed the ceremony for the renewal of her marriage vows with her husband of three decades. We raised kids in tandem—seeing them through their terrible twos and their terrible twenties—all without turning to drink, only because we took turns telling each other that "This too shall pass." I stayed in regular touch with her when her mother was dying, and she welcomed me into her house for months, twice, when I was determined to make major life changes against great odds. The first time, I was running away from a man who had discovered how to argue with his fist. The second time, I was trying to figure out how to come up for air, given the exhaustion of running a Zen Buddhist temple in an inner city.

But friendships, like everything else, change. Suffering is everywhere. The Buddha didn't mince words about this. At the same time he spent forty years teaching us, ad nauseum, how to not only survive but thrive in this ocean of heartbreak that he called samsara: through nonattachment.

Nonattachment doesn't mean that we don't care. We care. And it doesn't mean that we stop thinking about someone or that we lose our loving feelings for them. Nonattachment means that we let them be who they are, right now, and do what we have to do to be okay with that without trying to make them into anything else. This is where virya comes in. It can take an inordinate amount of energy to step back from wanting to call, write, email, twitter, or all of the above to this person to blame him or her for everything that we have both lost. It is just too easy to take the high road of righteousness, to write off the loss of the friendship to our expanding spiritual glow and their lack of one. If we can blame, we don't have to mourn. Virya allows us to mourn because it gives us what we need to stay smack in the middle of the loss.

This energetic effort is what allows us to let go of our opinions and wishes for how we want things to be. I'll be honest. This can totally suck. He was our best friend, after all.

Yet when we can muster the courage to simply be with the reality of our relationship as it is playing out right now, a funny thing happens. We get to keep the friendship in the form of memories and the feelings of caring. We see that what we have left is a shared history of growing up and learning how to live life, with all of its stories, laughter, and heartbreak.

There is great freedom in this place of virya, along with a boatload of tears. If we are willing to take this leap of acceptance, we'll discover that we get to keep this friend in our heart for ever and ever, with gratitude and goodwill. This is the friendship praised by the masters—one built on loving-kindness, compassion, equanimity, and (wait for it) joy. I promise.

THE RHINOCEROS CLUB

I love quirky clubs. When I was twelve it was U.M.A., Underground Monsters Anonymous. Those of us who were members bought silver charms that we had engraved with U.M.A. We hung the charms on bracelets or necklaces that we wore daily. Our only activity was to sneak out at night—you had to climb through a window—and roam through the neighborhood for a couple of hours until someone had to pee. Then we would all go home after voting on our next roam date. The club lasted until a police patrol car stopped to pick us all up and deliver us to our parents, who grounded us until we were thirteen. After that the club lost its allure.

These days I work hard to be a fine, upstanding member of the Rhinoceros Club. Its name comes from an old Chinese story in which a Zen master named Yanguan calls his attendant to bring him his rhinoceros fan. The attendant replies that it is broken. Yanguan says, "Well, if the fan is broken, then bring me back the rhinoceros." His attendant has no reply to this.[7]

What's a rhino? It's you and me. We get to replace the broken fan. We get to help each other so the world can keep spinning and we can all keep breathing. Members are the people who immediately go to the aid of someone who needs it, especially strangers. Added up, there are millions of rhinos, in spite of the fact that it takes energy and no small amount of courage to help someone you don't know. Just try handing some food or money out of your backpack to a big, burly fellow holding a sign that says, "Hungry and Homeless." The part of your brain that isn't flashing, "Bedbug warning! Bedbug warning!" combined with the part that is thinking, "This guy could beat the shit out of me if he wanted to" means that you're going to need some serious determination to move close enough to him to hand over an offering.

The more serious and immediate the need for help, the more virya is called for. One afternoon when I was driving through Los Angeles, a city I don't know at all, I saw a man fall out of his wheelchair across the street from where I was stopped at a red light. By the time I was able to turn around to get to him, two other people had stopped and lifted him back into his chair. Since I had found a parking spot I offered to push him the two blocks he needed to travel to get to his doctor's office. Within a minute the man looked up at me and said, "Slow down, girlie! I didn't pay for a plane ticket!" I was that pumped.

I've been the beneficiary of rhinos a handful of times in life-saving ways. Arriving in New York City from Sydney, Australia, as a teenager, I had no idea how to use the subway. Fearless and stupid, I tried to find my way from the Port Authority to midtown Manhattan, where I had a place to stay. I managed to get so lost that I ended up almost at the end of a line at night on a street of abandoned buildings with one dingy bar. The minute I walked into the bar I knew I was in trouble. It was smoke-filled and almost empty. It looked like there were a couple of prostitutes with their clients in the back booths. As a man approached me, a young woman popped out from behind the bar and asked me if I was lost. Completely, I told her. She spent hours taking me to the place where I was staying, using a combination of buses, the underground, and long walks through war zone neighborhoods. When we made it, she wouldn't take any money or even tell me her name. She just walked away as soon as she heard the buzzer that would let me into the building. A gold star rhino.

Another time I had just purchased my first car. I was thirty and living in Portland, Oregon. The car was one of those square Volvos with a stick shift. Having no idea how to drive a stick shift, I decided that the best way to learn was to take a road trip, the kind that would force me to learn how to change gears. Mountains would be good. I'd drive to Disneyland. There were lots of mountains on the way there. In spite of my theory I drove all the way to the California border before I perfected the art of shifting from first to second gear. After that, the shifting was easier, and I made it to Disneyland. On the way home, though, the car died, giving a long, quiet sigh before nestling onto the side of the road. I had very little money, no phone, and was in the middle of a desert.

Two cars later, a huge car pulled up behind me. The driver got out, a chocolate-skinned young man in an expensive-looking suit. He looked at the car and then at me.

"What happened?"

"My car is dead."

He nodded and told me to stay in the car and shift to neutral. Then he backed up behind me and proceeded to push me some sixty miles to the nearest gas station. When we got there I thanked him and said I couldn't believe he had done what he had done. It was his religion, he told me. It forbade him from passing anyone in need of help. Another gold star member of the club.

The Buddha taught that this kind of giving can bring great rewards to the rhino as well as to the person receiving the help. One time when he was in a town called Sajjanela, an upper-class Koliyan woman named Suppavasa made him a wonderful meal. When he was done eating it, he turned to her and said that by giving food to someone else, she was really giving four things: "What four? She gives long life, beauty, happiness, and strength. By giving long life, she herself will be endowed with long life, human or divine. By giving beauty, she herself will be endowed with beauty, human or divine. By giving happiness, she herself will be endowed with happiness, human or divine. By giving strength, she herself will be endowed with strength, human or divine."[8]

Even without the Buddha's promise, when we pay attention to our reactions to seeing people in trouble, we will notice our impulse to help. It is already there. Virya is the energy that outweighs the part of our brain that wants to make excuses for why we can't. When we help anyway, when we give the homeless man our peanut butter sandwich, or when we bring the abandoned dog home, there is a connection that happens. It feels like a spark of energy that moves through us to the other person or animal and from them to the next person and the next and the next, until suddenly we realize that not only are we upstanding members of the Rhinoceros Club but that we are frigging surrounded by rhinos. All we have to do is look.

4: Ease

....

Whoever dispels negative karma
through sincere spiritual effort
lights up the world indeed
He is the moon coming out
from behind the clouds.

The few who understand what is real,
like the handful of birds able to
escape
a trapper's net,
fly to the heavens.
—THE STILL POINT DHAMMAPADA[1]

....

HAVING KISSED MY ASS GOODBYE

ONE OF THE hardest things I've ever done as a dharma teacher was to preside, along with several other ministers, over the funeral of a teenager in Detroit. He was a young, charismatic scholar, loved by teachers and students alike. He was also gorgeous, a young Jesse Martin, complete with a world-welcoming grin and shiny eyes. Apparently, cheap heroin had hit the city, and he had tried some, his first. Most Detroit kids know not to try cheap heroin right when it comes into the city. To foster sales, it is usually of a higher than normal quality, too pure for someone unfamiliar with the game to use.

He took some at a high school party and was dead within hours. To their credit his parents grieved openly and publicly. And they opted for an open casket for his funeral. The entire school—students, staff, and teachers—was invited. The entire school accepted, filling a huge cathedral-sized church in the heart of the city.

From where I sat in front near the altar I was able to watch everyone's reaction to seeing his body. It was him. It looked like he was asleep, except his skin color was off, and it was too waxy. Some of the kids couldn't look, but most did. Their faces mostly showed shock. A few teared up. His best friend wept openly. All the adults cried.

It was a sweet, heartfelt, horrifying service. Detroit had lost one of its stars. Through it all, his mother was peaceful, calm, and comforting to everyone. She had an ease that made it possible for everyone else to recognize the shared heartbreak that had happened. None of us would ever be the same.

When I went back to my little room at the abbey following the service, I spent hours staring out at the street. While I had stared my own dying in the face several times, this was different. It was final. He was dead. And his mother was accepting of all of it, even though he, her only son, had been the light of her life. She held up the rest of us. I wondered how she could be so calm and present at the same time. How could a mother who had just lost her son to a terrible dying hold up the rest of us as she did?

For some reason her behavior reminded me of a conversation that the Buddha had with King Pasenadi when he first started teaching. Pasenadi had asked him if anyone is free from aging and death. Buddha's response? Nope. "The beautiful chariots of kings wear out. This body too undergoes decay."[2] He warned Pasenadi to take a good long look at how he was living his life, since aging and death were moving in on him. Pasenadi was freaked when this truth sunk in. What to do?

I decided that I wanted to feel what it was like to die. Taking up an old charnel ground teaching, where monks and nuns gaze at dead bodies as they decay, I pictured the young man's body and stayed with it for a long time. Then, painstakingly, I pictured my own body lifeless and decaying. Coming from an extended family where anxiety is the color of the day, I managed to terrify myself. Waves of nausea. I was faint. The main thing is that I stuck with the practice all night.

Just before morning, waves of understanding about all sorts of things started showing up. The first was that it doesn't make any sense to resist life as it is—acceptance is key. Then we can move out from there, to the place of "just this." This wasn't partial acceptance; it was complete acceptance. Aging and death are rolling in on all of us. And no amount of wealth, power, protection, or denial is going to save us. Actually nothing will save us. Okay! More understandings surfaced—flashes of the many personal foibles that continue to humble me, of the times I've been harmed and the people who have done the harming. It was a documentary that lasted for hours. A whole life that was asking for acceptance. Not understanding—acceptance.

I saw why Buddha had such a hard time waking up when he started out on his search for the cause of happiness. He was trying too hard. Starvation, sleeplessness, and physical pain didn't get him where he was hoping to go. Only when he eased up and relaxed into his meditation did his understanding come:

"He remembered an incident from his youth. Many years ago, when his father the Raja had ploughed the field with his own hand, he, Siddhattha, had been sitting at the edge of the field in the cool shade of a rose-apple tree, and had unexpectedly entered a state of aloofness from unwholesome states of mind, into a state of absorption (*jhana*) accompanied by thinking and pondering, delightful and happy."[3]

With this ease, his enlightenment gradually unfolded. While it may have been ecstatic, the most important aspect was its clarity. He saw that everything comes and goes, how interconnected everything is, how our grasping and craving lands us in shit every time.

He saw that aliveness is everything. And this aliveness is empathetic! We really are all in this together. And until we feel this empathy for ourselves, a miracle awaits. The world will be empathetic for us. It may not be in obvious ways until we start to watch, but when we do, we see it and feel it everywhere. It's in the air we breathe, on the ground where we walk, in the eyes of a mother who has just lost her son.

With empathy comes ease, the ability to just be with whatever it is that today has dished up. Maybe it will only be a bill we can't pay. Maybe it will be a mean text from someone who hasn't thought through his anger. Maybe it will be the death of our son. This boy's mother has given us the gift of a role model for reacting to all of it.

She has shown us how to not run away and how to care for each other even in the middle of the greatest heartbreak possible.

No Opinions, No Problem

My mother has more opinions per square inch than anyone I have ever known. I suspect that this mostly grew out of her experience as a teen watching Senator Joseph McCarthy going after public figures he decided were communists. His was a modern day witch-hunt to beat the band. She has always hated bullies. Here was one who was destroying lives, many through suggestion alone. And he was doing it with obvious pleasure. Mom still hates everything McCarthy stood for and thinks Richard Nixon was not only one of the worst presidents we've ever had the misfortune to elect, he was also one of the sneakiest, most cowardly, most pathetic people ever to have lived on this sweet planet. Just ask her.

When I was growing up, my experience of my mother was that with these strong opinions she was also a woman of great courage and integrity. She stood up to the nuns when they singled me out as a troublemaker in grade school. When I was a teenager her best friend for years was an openly gay man—this in a small conservative town in the hills of New England. They did everything together. She participates openly and eloquently in Internet debates about our nation's leaders, these days admonishing all of us who voted for President Obama to have more faith in the man. Tea Party people make her shake her head in disbelief. Conservative Christians? More shaking.

Her five children have mostly reflected her deeply held views. We are all quick judges of the behaviors and opinions that come out of thoughtless mouths. Our tendency, at least growing up, was to lump Republicans and conservative Christians in with racists and gay bashers and any other bullies who happened to find themselves in the media's limelight.

It was my karma to come of age professionally working for Republicans and conservative Christians. To my surprise, I found generosity, compassion, and kindness everywhere. A top partner in the firm I worked for quietly sponsored halfway houses for mentally ill adults across the country. Many of the accountants I worked with spent extra hours at night as well as lots of weekends doing pro bono work for everyone from Habitat for Humanity to domestic violence shelters.

Then came Zen. Then came the realization—way beyond any understanding—that we all have Buddha nature. That we all *are* Buddha nature. And that we all (psychopaths excepted) do our best for ourselves, yes, but also as much as we can for each other within the constraints of whatever greed, anger, and delusion we happen to be carting around internally. In other words, we all have an innate goodness that has our name on it. We all want our friends and our communities to be happy and safe. We want clean water and decent food for everyone.

One of the consequences of this realization has been a genuine eagerness to understand other religious traditions—what they teach and how people experience these teachings in their own lives. So, when two young friends invited me to their wedding at a huge conservative Christian church, I was thrilled. I got to be one of their witnesses, and I got to experience their tradition.

Tori and Jason were married on January 21, 2012. They are both adorable and huge hearted. Jason is a gifted healer, and if Tori could house the entire world in her backyard she would. Their church, Willamette Christian, is seriously Christian.

Jason and Tori's witnesses, hundreds of us, sang one of their wedding songs together at the top of our lungs. Many people held both hands in the air. The force of everyone's heartfelt energy made me cry. Singing, I was struck by how strong all of our yearning is for safety, and for the feeling of being loved. Safety and love were in that room. Safety and love *is* Jesus. The shared joy was palpable. And when Tori shouted, "I will!" to Jason's formal request for her hand, we all laughed, tears still falling. This place was love.

If I had been caught in opinions I would have missed the whole thing.

RESISTANCE FREE

When I think about the times in my life when I have been hangdog sad, the truth is my own thinking took me there. I would fill my mind with unease and anxiety and go to town. I would never be safe, loved, paid, or young again. Why me, Buddha? No, really, why me? Each time, the sadness was triggered by someone doing something hurtful out of thoughtlessness or maliciousness. Ouch. But then, after my initial reaction, what stretched the sadness out like miles-long taffy were my own thoughts, mostly about how things could have gone differently if the other person hadn't been such a jerk-and-a-half. When I've had the courage to really look at these thoughts, what I've seen is my own resistance to the truth of the situation. Maybe she shouldn't have acted that way. But she did. Maybe he shouldn't have lied. But he did.

Zen Master Seung Sahn used to teach that our words and speech are only thinking, and "Thinking makes suffering. You must throw them all in the garbage."[4] He taught his students, and they have been teaching me, "Don't know." In other words we need to let go of our resistance to the truth of a situation and let it be what it is. This doesn't mean that I've become a human lamppost for dogs and drunks to piss on. Instead it has led to a focus on what is going on right in front of me, "just this," without needing any editorial play-by-plays to make me out as something none of us are: invulnerable, all seeing, infallible. Don't-know mind has a way of opening up sufficient space so that I respond to whatever is going on without getting caught up in my own habitual reactions.

In Detroit, more than once, don't-know mind meant moving to the front of a crowd when an undermedicated paranoid schizophrenic decided that he needed to herd all of us into a safe place to protect us from the Catholics. I knew him pretty well, and he knew me. I got to say, "Hey, not before lunch! We have cookies!" It was always enough to relax him to where he could smile and tap back into enough reality to leave everyone else alone. In these moments there was no time to be scared or anxious or say to myself, "This should not be happening." The point was that it was happening.

Another time where nonresistance bailed me out of a difficult corner ended up with my apologizing to a huge room full of people. I suddenly realized that my humor was not only not a match for theirs, but it was potentially harmful. I was being a smart aleck about things they cared about. This was an apology to several thousand people. Again, right after I said something I thought was knee-slapping funny only to be met with silence, there was no place for resisting the response. They hadn't come for some bizarre Zen-laced comedy hour; they were meeting to try to establish a community dialogue, many under duress. The apology gave us all some breathing space.

Buddha's teachings have unerringly aimed us in the direction of complete acceptance of what is. That's what ease is all about. The more mindful we become through practice, the more obvious reality becomes. We discover that when we put energy behind our attention we notice all sorts of things: hesitation in a person's movement, an absence of smell in a room where someone is supposed to be dying, the suddenly changed color of our dog's paws. These things don't lie. We see more quickly when someone is sad, angry, or scared, or when a whole community is in trouble. As a result, less time and—to be blunt—fewer resources are wasted making things worse. Even responding with "I have no idea how to be helpful here" can be much more helpful than assuming we know what is best for everyone. This is an extremely difficult lesson for those of us who are born with genes that make us neurotic worriers—i.e., all of us.

When we hear stories of heroism, if we really study them, they are about this ability to completely be in a situation as it is, before responding with what is needed. Ironically there is great ease in the middle of such acts; the resistance is what exhausts us. I have a good friend who trained with a peacekeeper group back in the 1980s in Michigan. When she heard that a neo-Nazi group was planning a protest parade in downtown liberal Ann Arbor, she signed up to help keep the peace. When she got to the protest she discovered rage and hate on both sides of the street. The fury against the protesters was equal to their fury at all things liberal. Through her own clearheadedness about what was really going on, not only was she able to continue to stand in her designated peacekeeper position, but at one point, when the event turned violent, she was able to save the life of one of the protesters. Her team of three—an older white Buddhist female, a gay man, and an African American man—literally dragged the protester out of the melee to a street where he was safe. The irony of their act wasn't lost on any of us.

The peacekeepers didn't resist. They stayed alert and at ease and in so doing saved the day. Plus (you know I have to say this) resistance to the truth of any situation is futile anyway. There is no way any of us is going to checkmate reality. Seems a shame to keep trying.

GOODBYE, FLATTERY AND DECEPTION

My friend Jeffrey was a children's librarian for twenty-three years. People still stop him in the street to thank him for his story times and the written advice he constantly discovered for troubled parents. That he lasted for over twenty years is surprising to anyone who knows him well. Jeffrey does not suffer fools gladly. Working for a government agency, he was a fearless truth teller and—fortunately or not—never a flatterer.

What he is is clever. A lot of the time he frames his cleverness in fool's clothes. That way he can joke and tease the truth out of a situation, to everyone's benefit. My all-time favorite Jeffrey-as-fool story happened shortly after he joined the library. The institution's director was a wonderful man who had forgotten to retire. In his seventies, he was a figurehead holding a space that called for active leadership. Apparently nobody had it in him or her to tell him it was time to go.

Except Jeffrey.

At the end of one summer the library put on a huge celebration for all the kids who had participated in the summer's reading program. It was a medieval extravaganza, complete with medals for each participating child, a fool—Jeffrey, and a king—the library director. In his tights and vest, holding the fool's rod, Jeffrey was the epitome of ease, joking with everyone, including the director who he had started referring to as Nuncle. They had fun teasing back and forth until the end of the celebration, when Jeffrey turned to his boss and said, "You know, Nuncle, this would be a good time to go."

Two weeks later Nuncle retired. Maybe he was going to anyway. Maybe he just needed someone to have the courage to set flattery aside and say the truth out loud—that it was someone else's turn at the helm.

Buddha was no fan of flattery or deception. Both create tension, thick air. The opposite of ease. Buddha trained his followers in a kindness that was grounded in honesty, where no one was better than anyone else. One time a wanderer named Nigrodha landed in Rajagaha at the same time as Buddha. When the wanderer was scolded by a householder for his sloppy spiritual practice and his penchant for hanging out with a noisy crowd, Nigrodha turned on Buddha. As far as he was concerned, Buddha was the loser, not him: "The ascetic Gotama's wisdom is destroyed by the solitary life, he is unused to assemblies, he is no good at conversation, he is right out of touch." The Buddha heard this and decided to verbally spar with Nigrodha. He dismissed the arrogance of mendicants who pretend to themselves and others that they are better than the rest of us. Lying is just as bad: "Take the case, Nigrodha, of a self mortifier who practises a certain austerity. As a result, he is pleased and satisfied at having attained his end. And this is a fault . . . . He elevates himself and disparages others. . . . He has become intoxicated with conceit . . . ."[5]

This self-congratulatory way only grew worse when others flattered him. The next thing you know, the mendicant was getting picky about what foods he would eat and who he would spend time with. He started to get jealous when he saw someone else getting more respect. And he got just plain angry when he heard teachings that he considered to be below him. Things went downhill from there: "He is mean and spiteful, envious and jealous, crafty and deceitful, obstinate and proud, with evil desires and under their sway, with wrong views and given to extremist opinions; he is tainted with worldliness . . . ."[6]

Not good.

The Buddha offered a way out of the muck of flattery and deception: restraint. In this case an ascetic doesn't harm, or take what isn't given. She doesn't lie or crave sense pleasures. As a result, the teachings of mindfulness can aim the spiritual seeker in a more skillful and productive direction. In addition, when the need to be flattered disappears, compassion for others takes its place.

As Buddha's words sank in, Nigrodha was mortified. He saw his need to be flattered and how he deceived himself and others with a practice that hadn't led him anywhere near happiness. He was so upset that he asked Buddha if he would hear his confession. Yes. Given all of his mistakes, was there any chance that he would still be able to genuinely mature spiritually? Yes, again.

I am guessing that all the major religious traditions have teachings about flattery and deception and the need to let them go. In the Persian folk tradition, there is the story about a renowned and lovable character, Nasruddin, who, as he is walking through the marketplace carrying an expensive and fragile bowl, becomes so preoccupied gaping at everything around him that he trips on a rock, causing the bowl to fly in the air and crash to pieces. A small crowd gathers. Nasruddin carefully picks himself up, dusts himself off, looks at everyone for a minute and then asks: What are you looking at? Haven't you seen a fool before?

We all get to be fools sometimes. The Jeffrey version can heal the world. The Nigrodha version, not so much.

No Doubt

It seems like it takes a long time for westerners to trust our own spiritual efforts. I have no idea why this is. Maybe it's a cultural norm of putting our faith in the instructions of a religious leader, even when we've seen the harm done by religious leaders who are given carte blanche with the lives of their congregations. As a dharma teacher I regularly hear stories of deeply inappropriate behavior of my colleagues, from women and men. Ministers, priests, ministers again. Sometimes harming children, sometimes teenagers, sometimes postulants.

Even with such obvious harming, many of us keep following the rituals of the churches and their leaders. It takes moving a mountain to remove a minister or priest from his position, even in the face of unquestioned evidence that he has committed great wrongs.

For a long time I thought only I was hearing the stories of harm. I'm a female teacher, a grandmother, and relatively approachable.

But when I mentioned the pattern of stories to other teachers, they were hearing the same ones. Even in our own tradition people were giving away their capacity for telling right from wrong to unproven (to them) teachers. Talk about a formula for nervous breakdowns and worse.

The great irony, in Buddhism, is that one of Buddha's last teachings was to trust ourselves completely. He didn't say trust our teachers. He didn't even say trust the teachings. The job of a teacher is simply to point us in a direction. Ditto for the teachings. Our job is to find our own way. While this may not be as simple as following someone else's directions, it is necessary.

I was very lucky to have as a root teacher a Korean monk who forced me to trust myself early and often. The man is one tough cookie. He rages. He tantrums. He says terrible things about students who have parted ways with him, and almost all of us have. Without our tussles when I was his student I never would have thrived in Detroit; it was too raw. He pushed and pushed and pushed. At one point he said so many negative things about me after I left his community that I had an attorney send him a letter threatening libel. I was so furious at what I perceived as his harming the dharma (as though it could be harmed!) that I telephoned him to shout my piece. Not a proud moment, but there it is.

His response floored me. He heard me out and then responded that the Detroit sangha would be much stronger for my standing up to him. He was right; we were. He was reminding me to trust myself to the bone, and I have ever since. I have also come to believe that spiritual growth has a way of stalling out if we don't trust ourselves completely. Not in an arrogant way but by giving ourselves the gift of paying attention to our true-north antenna, the one that tells us when something is off. We tell ourselves, "It's okay" and "I'm doing just fine" every time we start to question ourselves. For most westerners, when we stay mindful and curious, this questioning happens sooner rather than later. A good teacher will corner us, will pit us against her in seemingly small situations until we can look her in the eye and say, "Nope. You're wrong." At Still Point this happened mostly in interviews with students. And every time someone told me or showed me I was incorrect, especially when they could do it without being angry or carrying a lot of past baggage, I was (mostly secretly) thrilled. Why? Because I knew that he was on his way.

When we don't doubt ourselves, then we don't doubt our spiritual path. In Buddhism, the eightfold path, Buddha's advice for how to live a life with great uprightness, follows our trusting ourselves quite naturally:

1. Right View: The knowledge of suffering, its origin, its cessation, and the path leading to its cessation.
2. Right Resolve: Turning away from excessive self-indulgence, for goodwill toward all beings, and for harmlessness.
3. Right Speech: Refraining from lying, slander, insult, and frivolous chatter.
4. Right Action: Refraining from taking life, from taking what is not given, and from sexual misconduct or excessive sensuality.
5. Right Livelihood: Giving up wrong ways of making a living, that is, through activities that harm or torment other beings.
6. Right Effort: Striving to prevent unwholesome mental states and overcoming those that have arisen. Likewise

striving to produce wholesome mental states and to maintain those that have arisen.

7. Right Mindfulness: Having put aside hankering and fretting for the world, contemplating body, feelings, mind, and mind objects, to bring under conscious control all processes and functions.

8. Right Concentration: Concentration whose aim is to cause the meditator to turn away from the world, to convey to him the experience of inner stillness, and to prepare his mind for higher insights.[7]

When there is no doubt, the eightfold path becomes our spiritual true north. It guides our efforts with or without a teacher nearby and keeps us safe and clear-headed. In this place of safety we discover that everything and everyone is our friend. Even the ones we need to escort to jail so they can stop harming innocents.

Again I See Bodhisattvas

I clearly remember the day I realized that you and I are completely surrounded by bodhisattvas. I was living in Portland. Every morning I would walk Bodhi the Dog to a city park about eight blocks away, usually well before dawn. There, clothes would be neatly laid out on three or four park benches. At first I thought someone living in the park was airing out the clothes. When I started to pay closer attention I saw that the clothes were different sizes and in really good condition. There were warm winter coats, scarves, and pants. Sometimes a skirt or dress showed up. It was one of the ways neighborhood residents were sharing with each other— anonymously and in the night.

Around the same time I noticed a kid who was always sitting on the curb in front of Powell's main entrance. If you didn't look closely, he was a teen waiting for some friends. If you did look, you saw that he was filthy. Usually he was pretty bruised up, as well. He was there for weeks. One day I saw a man—a clean-cut hipster who wasn't much older than the kid—kneel down beside him with a shoebox. The man pulled a pair of spanking new hiking boots out of the box. "I hope they're the right size."

When he proceeded to help the kid put them on, I looked up to see a small crowd who had stopped to watch. A few of us had tears in our eyes. It was such an unexpected gesture of pure kindness.

Except it kept happening. I love volunteering, which means I'm always on the lookout for a place to land. Sisters of the Road Café made its home a few blocks from me. Sisters feeds everybody. Mostly the everybody is made up of homeless and low-income folks who live within a few blocks of the place. Customers either pay a small amount for their meal or they can trade work for food. A handful of us were there to help prepare and serve the meals. I went through the volunteer training only to discover that there were way more volunteers than volunteer slots available. After my initial surprise, I was thrilled. Since then, the last three places where I've signed up have been oversubscribed by a lot.

When I lived in Michigan, almost ten years ago now, I remember being surprised whenever I saw more than one driver in a row giving handouts to someone holding a sign asking for help at a stoplight. These days it happens regularly—and in Eugene I see a dozen people holding signs every day.

The world isn't any better today than it ever was when it comes to anger, greed, and delusion. Yesterday a friend told me that there is more slavery in the world right now than there has ever been. The scale of the international sex trade is beyond imagining. Children—all over the world—who aren't kidnapped are sold into slavery by parents and family. Desperation can do that. Out of control doesn't even begin to describe the drug wars. With no signs of slowing down, the damage done by these heartbreaks calls for a universal response.

The thing is, we *are* responding. This doesn't mean that the problems will ever go away. My guess is they won't. But some things will get better and some lives will be saved because there are bodhisattvas willing to step up to the problems right in front of them. The kid needing shoes. The teenage girl needing a safe house. The country needing an attorney to help them take on the Khmer Rouge.

We say yes. And knowing that it isn't just me, or just you, creates an ease that doesn't exist when we feel too overwhelmed to respond. We are, each one of us, only one person after all. Knowing that millions of people, at this very moment, are offering time, resources, energy, and money to help others is deeply comforting and—surprise!—energizing. If my friend can sign up to take on bullies in the military, I can clean up the part of the neighborhood park that somehow keeps being forgotten by the city's cleanup crews. If my mother can stand in snowstorm after snowstorm with a sign saying "No More Wars," I can sign Amnesty International's petitions. If Food for Lane County can feed three hundred people a day in its free restaurant, I can leave a breakfast next to the van that is parked in the park each morning for the man who is living in it.

Last week on the way to the library, Bodhi the Dog and I stopped to give a fellow some packages of peanut butter crackers we had with us. When he saw what I was holding out of the car window he said, "Hang on to those, honey. I got plenty. Give 'em to the next fella you see. God bless."

Bodhisattvas are everywhere.

5: Joy

....

Truly we are happy.
Free of obstacles to happiness
we feed on joy.

Victory produces hostility,
because the ones who are defeated
live in grief.
Letting go of victory and defeat,
the tranquil mind lives
in happiness.
—THE STILL POINT DHAMMAPADA[1]

....

A DAY SAFE FROM ASTEROIDS

SOMETHING MARVELOUS happens when we wake up the day after we have officially kissed our butts goodbye. Joy is there. It typically comes in the form of a feeling of gratitude that is so strong there are no words. We can only weep. When we are able to get up and start our day we discover that we are noticing everything in our lives more deeply. How the light comes through the window in the front room. The sweet dog smell on an old quilt. The sound of soft wind moving through the tree next to the kitchen. The early morning cry of the *moktak*—a wooden fish—calling on everyone within hearing range to "wake up!" Colors are brighter. People glow so much we swear we can see their auras clearly. Could this mean a new livelihood in aura watching? Maybe we can watch out for bully auras in middle schools in order to forewarn innocents to tread lightly whenever they are in bullying range. Or, what the heck, watch for ill-intentioned people crossing national borders— offering a much cheaper method for protecting citizens than exists anywhere now. Maybe I've just had such a brilliant idea I need to stop typing and email the president about this right now. Then again, maybe not.

When I lived at Still Point Zen Buddhist Temple in Detroit I honestly thought I was about to be killed twice. The first time a man carrying a huge knife ran into me just as I walked out of the back gate to our meditation path and garden. We bumped hard enough to stumble back from each other. In that instant I watched him size me up head to toe, deciding whether to stab me. Then, in a blink, he made a decision to keep running.

The second incident was scarier. I was walking the eight blocks or so to the post office. To get there I had to walk past about four blocks of mixed housing—apartment buildings and single-family houses. Some of the buildings were kept up. Some were abandoned but still habitable. Some were war torn, with boarded up windows and porches that had been stripped of any usable building materials. Some of the buildings were basically the charred remains of what once was.

Beyond these blocks was a no man's land. The housing gave way to huge trashed lots. Even though the street I was walking on, Michigan Avenue, was a major thoroughfare in and out of the city, early on a Wednesday morning it was empty; I could have walked all the way to the post office down the middle of the street without seeing a person or a car. In a place like Detroit that kind of quiet isn't a good thing. No people meant no witnesses. If a crackhead—and there were plenty in the neighborhood—decided he or she didn't like the looks of me, I was in trouble. No people around meant nobody to ask for help or to go for help. Plus, I had forgotten my phone.

Getting to the post office was no problem. When I started to walk back to the abbey, though, a different scenario popped up in Technicolor. A man came out of one of the buildings behind me, a single-room-occupancy hotel. Out of the corner of my eye I saw him size me up. Then he looked up and down the street. Then he started walking toward me.

I was prey.

I just kept walking. When I picked up speed, he picked up speed. After a block I started to run. So did he. He almost caught up to me when I reached the blocks where there were some cars parked and some open windows. I kept running. He kept running. I think he was surprised that I was as fast as I was. All those races in my younger years were kicking in, laced with adrenaline.

He almost caught me. Then suddenly he stopped and turned around to walk back toward the hotel. By the time I made it to the abbey I was covered in sweat and shaking so much that I couldn't open the back door. Since I didn't get a good look at his face I couldn't do anything. The Detroit police, at least in those days, didn't have time for "I could have been killed by someone I can't describe" phone calls. Shrugging off the episode, I finished the day.

The next morning, hearing the morning wake-up chant, my first thought was, "I could be dead right now," followed by an exploding feeling of joy that I wasn't—that there was still time to do meditation practice, still time to watch my kids grow up, still time to play dharma teacher. For a long time after that, I sort of missed that energy shot of pure unadulterated joy. Then I realized that anything that reminds me of how fragile my life is can kick in a feeling of great joy when I also notice that we are all still here. Take asteroids, for instance. It is pretty amazing that we weren't hit last night by an asteroid while we were all sleeping. When you are done laughing at me, let me just remind you that in November 2011 an asteroid the size of an aircraft carrier made a close swing by Earth. It was the kind that could have wiped us out had it hit. In 1976 there was an equally close call. Another almost-hit is predicted for 2028. Although nobody, including me, appears to be particularly nervous about these massive space travelers, just thinking about the damage they can do and waking up knowing we haven't been hit can trigger gratitude, the kind that opens our hearts to joy.

For those of us unwilling to consider the miracle of an asteroid-free day, it turns out that any level of gratitude has the capacity to spark joy. Small things, even silly ones, are triggers: the smell of bread baking, Ellen's jokes, a snail mail letter, new buds on a tree. And until gratitude for small things stirs up joy, thinking about near misses from asteroids and crackheads wanting your lunch money will work.

The Lotus Sutra's Formula for a Happy Life

Joy is a sweet feeling of gladness and delight. I miss it when it isn't around, and it hasn't been in the air for a while now. It feels like something happened to all of us over the course of this last great recession. We forgot about joy. Instead our focus has been on pleasure—the pleasure of parties, drinking, social networking, sex. While I think of most pleasures (with a few exceptions) as great fun, they tend not to unfold as joy. That night of drinking, rushing around to shop for exactly what we want, checking in with each other via text after text, all unfold as busyness or fodder that fills our days. Pleasurable fodder, perhaps, but not joy.

This is a huge loss. We've lost the feeling that delight can bring to our bodies, hearts, and minds when we give it time to sink in. We've lost the feeling of security and comfort that comes with gladness. We've lost the power joy has to open our hearts and minds to the wondrous reality that surrounds us—and is us.

How do we get joy back? It turns out that we don't need to get anything back. We just need to acknowledge the joy that is always right here. The Lotus of the True Doctrine Sutra is a treasure trove of teachings that can lead us back onto a joy track. The sutra, which appeared in the third century A.D., is basically a discourse that Buddha gave toward the end of his life at Vulture Peak. He told his audience that there are three vehicles that will carry us to enlightenment. The first one is the act of hearing the teaching of the Buddha himself. The second is our own effort. The third is the path of the bodhisattva, where we vow to be helpful to all beings for ever and ever, amen. Faith in the vehicles is important. So is faith in ourselves. In our time, Zen Master Seung Sahn used to teach his students that all enlightenment means is a one hundred percent belief in our true self, or buddhahood. Not ninety-nine percent, not ninety-eight percent. This is the kind of faith that the Lotus Sutra calls for.

Back on Vulture Peak, Buddha reminded his followers that everything he taught would help them. He then offered stories to drive home the importance of this faith in ourselves and the teachings. In one parable, a man goes to a friend's house, parties hard, and passes out drunk. His friend gets called away, but before he leaves he ties a priceless jewel into the man's garment as a gift. The man is sleeping so soundly he doesn't know anything of this. When he wakes up, all he knows is that his friend is gone. He gets himself up, cleans himself off, and goes off to see the world, trading his labor for room and board. In those days, hard labor meant doing jobs like digging wells with primitive tools or removing huge boulders from fields. He just barely manages to earn enough to keep himself in food and clothes.

Years later he meets his friend again when he shows up asking for work. His friend can't believe his eyes. The guy is a wreck. His friend tells him that years ago he sewed a priceless jewel into his garment so he'd never have to worry about making a living: "I formerly in such a year and month and on such a day tied a priceless jewel within your garment. Now as of old it is present there and you in ignorance are slaving and worrying to keep yourself alive. How very stupid! Go you now and exchange that jewel for what you need and do whatever you will, free from all poverty and shortage."[2]

Joy is that gem. It is always right here, right now. The great irony is that when we don't feel joy or don't think we deserve it are those times when we have filled every minute with our personal melodramas. We are drowning in our I-me-my worlds. When we have the courage to just stop and consider that Buddha may have been on to something, we give joy some space to sparkle. When I was thrashing about in the Maitreya Buddhist Seminary, I sometimes got completely caught by a feeling of failure when it came to the things we were learning. I couldn't memorize the chants to save my life. I couldn't be quiet all day without sneaking out to the backyard to joke around. I couldn't sous chef without creating a tornado-sized mess on the kitchen floor. Sometimes Sunim would catch me mid disaster and say, "P'arang, you are Buddha." For a long time I thought he was saying, "You are Bob." I wondered who Bob was and whether he ever made it through the torture of the seminary. Then I read the Lotus Sutra and realized that he had been saying Buddha, not Bob. The gem was there all the time. I had it in me to learn the chants, keep my mouth shut, and cut vegetables without creating a mess. So I did.

Joy is that gem. As we start to believe that we deserve joy in our lives, a funny thing happens. We start to figure out what will help us feel it. Even just thinking about joy starts the ball rolling. Simply finishing the sentence, "Joy is . . . ." can work wonders because it kick-starts a sort of watching. We start to notice where small shivers of joy still pop up in our busy lives, begging to be noticed. And we notice who and what feeds that shiver. For any of us who have a hard time knowing how to complete the joy sentence, a foolproof trigger is the *Sound of Music*'s formula: raindrops on roses and whiskers on kittens. Images of roses and kittens can crack through the hardest of hearts if you believe. And on this path, belief is mandatory.

WITHOUT HASTE

On January 2, 1200, a baby boy was born to a court courtesan and Lord Kaga Michichika, a direct descendant of a famous tenth-century emperor in what is now the city of Kyoto, Japan. The baby's father died when he was two years old. His mother died when he was eight. The boy went on to become one of the most precocious monks in Zen history: Dogen. From his childhood on, Dogen was obsessed with wanting to experience reality as it is, and not through ordinary eyes. His intensity probably drove most of his teachers nuts, given how many he had burned through by the time he was a young man. Finally, when he was in his early twenties, a monk named Myozen allowed Dogen to accompany him to China to study there.

They sailed from the port of Hakata to the land of Sung in 1223. When the Japanese monks landed, an old monastery cook showed up at the ship to buy some Japanese mushrooms they had on board. When Dogen asked him to stay and chat, he declined, saying he needed to get back to the monastery to cook for the next day. Dogen argued that surely there were other cooks who could cook for the monastery. That was true, replied the old man, but it was his job to be head cook. Not only that, his work *was* his Zen training. How could he leave that to others?

Dogen kept pushing. What about meditation? What about studying koans? Wasn't he wasting his life working in the kitchen? The old man laughed because he knew that doing whatever is right in front of us, whether that is cooking or cleaning or breastfeeding a baby, *is* our spiritual work—*is* Zen. And when we finally give in to this truth and fully concentrate on what is right in front of us, Zen offers up a great surprise. Joy arises. It comes with the concentrated effort and focus. No need for a monastery. No need for a teacher. Simple, quiet, concentrated effort opens the magic door. There's a catch, of course. The catch is that we can't rush.

It's almost like a game. If we try to do anything else, or if we rush, the joy doesn't surface. But if we find our own natural, unhurried form of concentration on what is right in front of us, we crack open what every one of us yearns for: happiness.

The problem most of us have with this simple formula is that we've been raised to act in opposite ways. We're rewarded for our drive, our achievements, our gift for juggling many things at once. Ever the good student of this Western paradigm, when I was in third grade I set my life's goal: to give a million dollars away to poor people. I even wrote it down in my secret diary, the one with only one key, a key I scotch taped to the inside of my underpants every day so my snoopy little sisters couldn't read my secrets. From that point on, I was driven. Even at the age of eight I knew that giving away a million dollars meant that I needed to earn more than that. This in turn meant I had to ace classes and be gifted at extracurricular stuff. School president would be a start. An Ivy League education? Also helpful. A doctorate in a tough subject would open doors to jobs that paid well.

I raced through all those things until, at the ripe old age of thirty, I was giving away—ta-da—at least $250,000 a year. While it wasn't exactly my own money, I had a significant say in where and how funds were spent in the form of grant recommendations. By then I also had the nickname Hurricane. The rushing continued through my love affair with the private sector and into the seminary. Fortunately at that point I hit a wall in the form of a huge young monk who had a talent for stepping in front of me to shout, "Slow down!" whenever he caught me rushing from one task to another. Sunim also proved to be skilled at breaking my habits by instructing me to perform the same mundane tasks over and over until I got them right. Bathrooms had to be rescoured ad nauseum, top to bottom. Painting jobs like doors and fences? I lost count. It took years for me to slow down to where I could focus on one thing at a time and enjoy it.

But when I did, I was transfixed by the beauty of the world and of people. I had been completely missing it. I discovered nuances in colors. I discovered that every person has a story and that every story is not only fascinating but heartbreaking. I discovered the broken feeling that comes with loss, something I had completely ignored growing up. Who had the time? And I discovered genuine love—the patient, compassion-filled, how-can-I-help? version.

I found that joy is everywhere and is dumbfoundingly accessible. When Monkey the Cat leans over to smooch Bodhi the Dog on the couch, joy. Watching four weather fronts fly through Eugene in the course of an afternoon—snow, rain, hail, sleet—joy. Dogen's teacher was onto something big. The slower and more mindful I am at what I'm doing, the greater the joy. It turns out that cooking meals from scratch offers a perfect trigger. Here is a recipe that has never let me down:

BAKED POTATO CHOWDER

3 or 4 big russet potatoes

3 or 4 slices of pretend bacon

1 big onion, chopped mindfully

1 big green pepper,
chopped the same way

2 stalks of celery,
chopped you know how

4 cups of vegetable
(or chicken) broth

1 cup of milk or soy milk or,
if it's your fancy, sour cream

Bake the potatoes at 400 degrees for one hour. Pierce them first so they don't explode in the oven. It's okay to coat them in a little olive oil if you want. Fry the bacon and chop it up mindfully. Saute onion, pepper, and celery in a big pan that has been lightly greased with a little vegetable oil. Add broth and milk. Bring to a boil. Add chopped up potatoes after they are done baking. Throw everything except the bacon into a blender. Reheat if the chowder isn't warm enough and then serve, topped with crumbled bacon bits.

This is supposed to serve four people but I've never made it past two, especially if it's the whole meal (and you've had to taste as you go, in true chef fashion).

NO PLACE FOR THE TIMID

Not many people know that Shakyamuni Buddha was a skillful marriage counselor. He was married for thirteen years, after all. So he knew how difficult relationships were for his followers, from King Pasenadi to the people who showed up for his teachings during his visits to their villages. As a result he often worked domestic themes into the lessons he offered. On one occasion, when he was staying in the Bamboo Grove's Squirrel Sanctuary at Rajagaha, he spotted a young man, Sigalaka, bowing in six directions—to the east, south, west, north, sky, and earth.

Buddha asked him what he was doing. The young man's response was that when his father was on his deathbed he had asked him to pay homage to the six directions: "And so, out of respect for my father's words, which I revere, honor, and hold sacred, I have got up early to pay homage in this way . . . ."[3]

The Buddha looked at him for a while and then told him that he wasn't really paying homage. The young man was pretty surprised and not a little put off. He asked Buddha what he would consider to be a proper way. Buddha replied that the real six directions that need to be honored and protected are the mother and father (east), teachers (south), wife and children (west), friends and companions (north), ascetics and brahmins (zenith), and servants, workers, and helpers (nadir).

Then, more explicit instructions. A man honors his partner by being faithful, by not disparaging her, and by providing her with adornments (which these days could be anything from jewelry to lotion to a new meditation robe). Buddha went on to say that a wife who is kind, faithful, careful with foods, and skilled and diligent "in all she has to do" creates for her partner a relationship that is both peaceful and free from fear.[4] In these ways we remember how precious our partners are and better demonstrate our reflections of this preciousness.

In another story, Buddha was traveling along the path between Madhura and Veranja when a number of couples asked him for relationship advice. He started out with the bad news. Any husband who destroys life, takes what isn't given, engages in sexual misconduct, speaks falsely, indulges in intoxicants, is stingy, or makes fun of ascetics and brahmins is no better than a wretch. If his wife has the same characteristics, she is also a wretch and theirs is a doomed relationship. If one of them is a wretch while the other one is of good character, generous, and respectful, such unevenness of character can also cause problems.

The way out is what Buddha called a god living with a goddess.

In this case they both honor life, abstain from intoxicants, and are virtuous, generous, and respectful. No place for the timid, but there it is. In this place, joy happens.

The way to get to the god and goddess part? A combination of ethics and mindfulness. In all the years that I have been a dharma teacher I've found that most couples have the ethics part down. In spite of tabloid reports, most partners are faithful, try hard to be good people, and play well with others. Most of us aren't addicted to an intoxicant, or if we are we know it and are doing something about it. Where we get into trouble is in the places where we forget to pay attention. This is where the small can transform into gigantic in the blink of an eye: A partner who consistently spends more than the budgeted amount for weekly groceries. Someone who is habitually late for dinner. A wife who wants to talk about "our problems" when it's clear that her husband is exhausted after a long hard day of looking for employment. On the surface these aren't deal breakers. But it only takes one scratch below that surface to see how deeply a partnership has been harmed.

The need for the fire of attention takes on a whole new meaning when we realize that one of our small habits is actually eroding our marriage. This fire of attention also helps because it can spotlight possible compromises we can make for the god or goddess we are living with: calling home to say we'll be late, saving relationship conversations for weekend mornings when we aren't so rushed, buying groceries with cash so we can't buy more than we have budgeted for. Where I live we all clean bathrooms, wash sheets, and cook. Sometimes we're god. Sometimes we're goddess. With every chore that is done well, joy grows—for everyone.

THE END OF SEARCHING

When George Clooney was asked his idea of perfect happiness in a *Vanity Fair* interview, he answered, "Laughter." When we laugh we're happy. Try it. It's impossible to be anything but happy when we are in the throes of a good belly laugh. In this place is the end of suffering. If we could put ourselves on pause in the middle of a good laugh, what we would find is a clearheaded okayness, with a dusting of what feels like hope but is really trust in things exactly as they are.

Zen includes much laughter. One of the first dharma talks I remember hearing included this joke: Four friends wanted to practice Zen together. They decided to do a seven-day silent retreat up in the mountains. It started off okay. At the end of the first day, the room grew dim. Someone said, "We should fix the lamps." Someone else responded, "Shhh. Don't you remember we made a vow of silence?" The third friend: "Won't you two be quiet?" The fourth: "It looks like I'm the only one around here who knows how to be quiet."

They looked at each other and roared.

The point is that once we've admitted to ourselves that we've found a path that suits us, our job is to relax and just do the work. Laughter at our foibles grows because we see that in the end we're all pretty silly.

There was always laughter at Still Point. We laughed at the antics of the temple cat, starting with her insistence that we leave her alone on a meditation cushion when we went into the meditation hall to sit. We laughed at how we would get caught in the loop of a chant, only getting out when we just plain stopped singing. We laughed when our meditation pants fell down because we caught a trouser leg on a heel while we were doing prostrations. We even laughed at some of our Buddhist names; "Withered Willow Tree" is still my favorite. Almost always, when someone nailed a koan in an interview, we laughed together, mostly because koan responses can be so obvious. We miss them until finally we don't.

All this in the middle of a city filled with heartbreak. The laughter didn't make the heartbreak go away. Instead it somehow kept our heads clear so we could do what we could to be helpful to the community. Sometimes this meant driving someone to an emergency room. Sometimes it meant sweeping the walks. Sometimes it meant keeping baby chickens warm enough to hatch.

Shakyamuni Buddha could be hilariously funny. One time, when he finally decided that it was time to go home to visit his family after years of being away, Buddha braced himself. He had abandoned the whole lot of them, after all. His father lost his successor. His wife lost her husband. His son lost his father. His father greeted him with an armload of crankiness. Not only had his son been gone for years but when he showed up not only was he not wearing princely garments but he had the audacity to show up in monks' robes, begging.

They argued in front of a huge crowd—his father scolding him for his behavior and dress, with Buddha arguing back that he was a monk who was doing exactly what he should be doing. It didn't take long for his father to build up such a head of steam that he couldn't even hear his son and just kept yelling. Buddha finally decided, Okay, time for a miracle. And proceeded to lift up into the sky, where he put on his own private fireworks display. His father was silenced. What we do to win arguments.

How is it that the end of searching starts with laughter? The best I can come up with is that once we've admitted to ourselves that we've found a spiritual path that supports us, the deepest part of us relaxes so we can do the work of maturing our understanding of how we fit into the world. Laughing at our mistakes—and we all make them—allows us to keep going and keep our efforts light. We learn to not take ourselves so seriously. We learn to leave room for wisdom—as opposed to intelligence—to surface. We learn the truth of our interconnections and how one of the fastest paths from heart to heart is shared humor.

Gentleness

Gentleness is a particular form of kindness, one that is free of harshness, sternness, and violence. You can see it everywhere in the animal world. YouTube is full of videos celebrating the gentle behavior of dogs in the face of crawling children and scratching cats and mama cats licking their babies clean.

Nature can be gentle. April, at least in the northwest, tends to leave like the lamb March promised. Our spring here is soft, filled with tiny buds that get bigger by the day and birdsong that fills the sky.

There are lots of examples of Buddha's gentleness in the ancient sutras. In one story he is walking down a narrow street and a dung collector is walking toward him. This is a man who has the job of collecting excrement in containers, which he then carries to the outskirts of the city. When the man sees Buddha coming toward him, he is mortified. Unfortunately he is blocked in. Buddha approaches him, rests a hand on his shoulder, and quietly asks him if he would like to become a monk. When he says yes, the man is welcomed into the sangha as an equal to all the other monks.

Another time Buddha knows he has eaten food that has gone bad. Rather than say anything publicly, knowing the sacrifices his host has made to make the meal, he quietly pulls his attendant Ananda aside and instructs him to make sure nobody else eats the spoiled dish.

As I thought about gentleness, it occurred to me that it may have become a lost art in modern society. This would be a tragedy, because where there is gentleness, there is ease. And where there is ease, there is joy. But it was hard to come up with examples of gentle behavior. Maybe, I told myself, we just aren't gentle anymore. I decided that the only way to tell what our modern state of gentleness is would be to do a survey. Completely unscientifically I walked around with a tiny green notebook in my back pocket for thirty days, vowing to jot down any and all person-to-person gentleness sightings. After thirty days I had nothing. Concerned, I wrote to my friend Pauline for advice. She is a former Catholic nun who has a sixth sense about these sorts of things. Her response was to suggest that gentleness is probably found behind closed doors. That made sense. In the hermitage there is lots of gentleness around on a daily basis. To double-check myself, I wrote to my friend Kassapa in Minneapolis, as well. What advice did he have? Is public gentleness a thing of the past?

This was his response: "P'arang, Here are some suggestions for finding gentleness: Ride a city bus. Walk through a county hospital.

Look at the simple way a family with children eats at a restaurant. Watch dogs in a dog park. The way a daffodil serenades the day. Or squirrels interact or birds feed their young. Or a tree's shade creates relief from the rain or the sun."

I was missing something. So, I plunked myself down to watch without a time limit. And there it was. Eugene's river walk park has a huge playground in its middle, with lots of slides and things to crawl on, under, and in. Stopping to rest on a bench one morning, I overheard a young father trying to get a job interview on his cell phone. He was polite but persistent. The person on the other end wasn't budging, though, so after a couple of minutes I heard, "Well, thank you for your time." I could feel his disappointment and worry. Just then his little boy, maybe three, trying to climb up one of the slides the wrong way, tripped and fell over its side. He was more shocked than hurt. I started to get up to help, but his dad was way ahead of me. He ran over to his son, brushed him off, and said something like, "That was a close one, huh?" Then he sat down on the wet sand, the little boy in his lap, and just rocked him gently, brushing his forehead. The boy calmed down and looked up at his dad, grinning and relieved. They nose nuzzled, and when his father looked up, I saw it. Joy. Against all odds, joy.

6: Concentration

....

The immediate condition for the arising of wisdom is
concentration. As the Buddha often says: "Develop concentration,
monks. One who is concentrated sees things as they really are."
To "see things as they really are" is the work of wisdom;
the immediate basis for this correct seeing is concentration.
—BHIKKHU BODHI[1]

....

BUDDHA IS GRASS SHOES

CONCENTRATION IS the faculty of the mind that makes it possible for us to hold our attention steadily on one thing. Even in the time of Shakyamuni Buddha, concentration was difficult. He compared people's minds to elephants when they are in rut—in a word, uncontrollable. And yet we need to learn how to concentrate if we are going to mature spiritually. Throughout his years of teaching, Buddha gave many instructions on how to move from elephant-rut mind to quiet concentration. He was so effective a teacher that even the gods would listen.

In one city, Nadika, when Buddha was expounding on the rebirths of some of his followers who had died, a crowd of gods showed up. When they were asked why they'd come, one of them, Brahma Sanankumara, said they were so pleased by how accessible Buddha's teachings were that they learned from him as well. In particular he liked it that Buddha taught his followers how to develop and perfect four kinds of concentration: concentration of intention accompanied by effort of will, concentration of energy, concentration of consciousness, and concentration of investigation.[2] Even better, he started people out with a teaching of how to begin and then how to build on our own experience: the eightfold path of right view, right thought, right speech, right action, right livelihood, right effort, right mindfulness, and right concentration. How does it work, you may ask? According to Buddha, from right view (understanding impermanence and interpenetration) arises right thought. From right thought arises right speech. From right speech arises right action. From right action arises right livelihood. From right livelihood arises right effort. From right effort arises right mindfulness. From right effort arises—ta da—right concentration. From right concentration arises right wisdom, and from right wisdom arises right liberation.

So living a life that is moral—from our thinking to our actions and how we earn our living—is key to being able to concentrate. When we meditate we can see how this works for ourselves. For example, when I've had cross words with someone, stepping off the cliff of right speech into wrong speech, trying to meditate later is futile. I find my mind wanting to go over everything that was said, ad nauseum. Usually I start out rationalizing why I was right in the situation. Then I get caught in the loop of feeling remorse for my unskillfulness. Then the whole meditation period is lost to impatience because I am eager to apologize so we can get past the discomfort of disagreement. Add the unskillful thoughts that we are all prone to, our unskilled actions, and poor choices of livelihood, and it's a wonder that any of us can concentrate on anything.

Because this was painfully clear to Buddha, he gave us the homework of the eightfold path. If we clean up our choice of livelihood, concentration gets easier. When we monitor our actions to be as harmless as possible, concentration improves. The quieter we are—the more we give up idle chitchat, gossip, and old, tired arguments—the easier the concentration. All of this can be easily tested through our own experience.

Within this framework of a moral life, a wonderful reward awaits us. It turns out that whatever we concentrate on helps us to wake up. During meditation, for example, we can *mu* or count our breaths or ask ourselves a question like "What is this?" We can concentrate on a single word like *yogurt* or *juice* or *sunshine*. There is a funny story in Korean Zen about a monk named Sok Du who asked his teacher, "What is Buddha?" Apparently he wasn't the smartest banana in the bunch. On the other hand, he had concentration down to a fine art. His teacher responded that "Buddha is mind," but Sok Du thought his teacher said, "Buddha is grass shoes."

For three years he concentrated on the phrase. Buddha is grass shoes. Buddha is grass shoes. Buddha is grass shoes. One day when he was carrying some firewood down a hill he tripped on a boulder sticking out on the path and tumbled down the hill. When he stopped, he suddenly woke up! Everything in the universe is one thing, and one thing is everything in the universe. He was thrilled.

When I was formally teaching, a student asked if he could use the phrase "Jesus is God" for his concentration practice. I was happy that he had a phrase that appealed to him. At the same time I was a little concerned that it would set up a Christian-versus-Buddhism tension in him. It didn't. Instead he flew through every koan I offered to him and ended up being a shining example of wisdom and compassion. So first we do the prework: deciding to be serious about our spiritual practice. The eightfold path then gives us the path to tread from there on out. Then we choose the phrase or word that helps us to really concentrate on our practice. Then we gnaw on it. Repeat, repeat, repeat. We repeat until one day we find ourselves laughing out loud because Buddha has been grass shoes all along.

ORANGE WALNUT SALAD

There is no question that concentration is key to waking up. Not the kind of concentration that you see on a frustrated little kid's face when he is trying to make a Lego superhero with all the wrong Legos. This concentration is lighter, a constant and calm focus where everything around us and inside of us is quiet and still. Seung Sahn used to teach that correct concentration is a one-pointed mind that doesn't want anything beyond what is right in front of us. In other words, we pick a focus and stay there.

The coffee shop I am sitting in, Allann Brothers, is a Eugene institution. It is also my neighborhood coffee shop. I love to stop by, post meditation, to quietly sip tea among the coffee crowd. It's a happy place. The music is invariably from an old rock station. The baristas know my face. By 9 a.m. every seat in the place is taken, even the two black chairs in the corner that face a fingerprinted window dusty enough to appear curtain-covered.

About four of the twenty or so tables have two or three peo-ple chatting together quietly. The rest? Headphones and laptops or iPads. I'm the only person with tea and the only person who is actually listening to Fleetwood Mac singing about thunder and rain. It occurs to me that—as a culture—we may have forgotten how to concentrate. Too much comes at us too constantly. I can feel it in myself following a visit with my own computer's windows to check in on family, friends, and the world at large. For about a half hour afterward I find it impossibly hard to focus on one thing. My brain lines up various, mostly unrelated topics it wants to explore further next time, just because. Why are sloths the way they are, anyway? You get the idea.

It turns out that relearning how to concentrate can be great fun. All we need to do to remember, or to taste genuine concentration for the first time, is to find a task that pulls in as many senses as possible—sight, hearing, taste, touch, and smell. And then we simply do the task from beginning to end. Examples of the kind of tasks that can work here are learning a new song on a musical instrument or weeding a yard—especially in the spring when the weeds aren't obvious.

Cooking a new recipe does the trick for me every time. But there are ground rules. Music can't be on. The phone needs to be off and in a different room. Idle chitchat needs to be at a standstill. Pets, partners, and kids need to hang out somewhere else. Then all you have to do is pull out a recipe you've been meaning to try, collect its ingredients, and make the meal, start to finish. Orange Walnut Salad is one dish that never fails to kick me into a one-pointed focus. For some reason it always feels like the first time I'm mak-ing it. I like to pretend that it's the last thing I'll ever make in this lifetime so it needs to be perfect. This pretense slows me down enough to pay close attention to each task. I know I've hit concentration heaven when making the salad feels suspiciously like a ballet. The bonus? The salad is delicious every time.

ORANGE WALNUT SALAD

1 head of romaine lettuce, cleaned and broken into bite-sized pieces

1 to 2 handfuls of fresh spinach, also cleaned and broken into bite sized pieces

Put them both into your favorite big bowl.

2 oranges, peeled and broken into teaspoon-sized pieces that are then squished (by hand) onto the lettuce and spinach bits. I throw the orange bits right into the salad. No sense wasting good fruit.

By now, smell, sight, hearing, and touch should be in high gear. Your home will be smelling like a tropical island, your taste buds will be awake with citrus, and you'll be painfully aware of any finger cuts or thorn stabs on your hands.

½ cup of walnuts, chopped

I put mine in a paper bag and stomp on them, saving the bag for another use later. Mix the walnuts into the bowl with everything else.

For the dressing, mix:

½ cup of the best olive oil you can afford (If you can't afford any, a vegetable oil will work.)

¼ to ½ cup vinegar, preferably red wine (Again, if you can't afford it, any vinegar will work.)

½ teaspoon salt (Don't leave this out.)

½ teaspoon any kind of mustard

Dump them all into the bowl and mix with your hands. Wash your hands. Serve the salad. Try to share it if you can.

* *

If you have been concentrating, it will taste like one of the most delicious meals you've ever had. Even the first taste, with all its flavors playing with each other, will make you understand why Proust could have written his life story coming off of a bite of a cookie. There will be a calmness and even a feeling of grace. That's what concentration does. If you find you don't have any of these feelings, I'd try the salad again on a day when you've had more sleep. Sooner or later, with practice, concentration will kick in— the kind you can ride all the way to awakeness.

Scrubbing down the kitchen floor can have the same effect if you don't feel like cooking.

GILGAMESH'S CAR

When I think about how I yearn for BBC specials, I wasn't surprised to hear that some monks turn on tiny television sets in the mountains of Korea after lights out. It is our shared hunger for stories. When we pay attention, all stories teach us something. Some teach about heartbreak. Some teach about perseverance. Some about how there continues to be good in the world. They teach us about the seven factors of enlightenment—about mindfulness and curiosity and energetic effort and ease and joy and equanimity. They also teach us about concentration.

The epic of Gilgamesh is one of those stories. It appeared somewhere around 2600 BCE, was copied and studied for two thousand years, and then was lost until recently. (In the Buddhist tradition, two hundred years ago counts as recently.) The story is about how a young punk is transformed into a good king through a combination of adventures and heartbreak. When Gilgamesh's best friend, Enkidu, is killed because they've decided to take on an enemy that is way too huge to beat, Gilgamesh sits beside him for seven days, incoherent with loss. He then becomes completely freaked. If his friend could die as a young man, could he? We all know the answer. Gilgamesh becomes consumed with the knowledge that his death is certain. He just doesn't know when it will take place. His obsession with his own dying becomes the "car" he surrounds himself with—and he rides it everywhere. Although he discovers that his life will last much longer than his beloved Enkidu's, his constant knowing that death could happen at any moment triggers a deep concentration in him. He learns to completely focus on whatever is happening in his life—good and bad, happy and sad. He discovers, as we all do when we admit to ourselves that death could happen at any time, that all we have is right now. For Gilgamesh, this means that he becomes skilled at shrugging off the small stuff and figures out that pretty much everything is small stuff. Melodramas? Who has time? Instead he focuses on honing the virtues of a good leader, evolving into a character for whom everything that happens is okay in its own way. A crisis hits? Okay. A new lesson in humility? Okay.

It turns out that Gilgamesh's journey to understanding the value of knowing that death is near is our own. Maybe we only have one more day to live. Okay. Maybe our partner dies. Okay. Or our child. Maybe nobody will ever be kind to us again. Okay. This okay of acceptance takes great concentration energy, because it demands of us that we stay in the moment to be able to cope. All the more reason to practice concentration whenever possible, because we'll need it soon if we don't already.

About eight years ago one of my dharma brothers, in his early thirties at the time, came home to the abbey from a day job pretty upset. He told me that one of the men he was working with on a construction site had a huge lump growing out of his forehead just over his eye. It was so big that it was actually pushing his eyeball out of its socket. Since he didn't have any health insurance he hadn't gone to see a doctor. Suddenly he was in intensive care in the city's hospital, dying. Could I visit?

I did. At first the young man didn't want anything to do with me. He was pissed at everything—the world, the doctors, his mother. I'm guessing I reminded him of her—bossy and old. I asked if it would be okay if I just sat with him. A nod yes. Having no idea what to do and not a little unnerved by the huge growth, I could only concentrate on my breathing. In and out. In and out. In and out. After a while he looked over at me.

"I'm dying."

"I know."

We sat together in silence. Then he looked at me again.

"What should I do?"

"I don't know."

More sitting. More quiet. By now I was weeping. This felt like such an unnecessary death. For some reason I thought about

Gilgamesh. Maybe because when I finally had the guts to actually see the man beyond the bulge, I saw that he was young and beautiful. Strong. Fit. Finally I asked him, "Can you make it okay?"

"Fuck no."

But he asked me to come back. At the abbey we chanted our hearts out for him, putting his name in the lap of the Buddha statue on the altar. When I went back to the hospital two days later, he was dead. The nurse who told me said, "He was okay with it at the end."

I wept anyway.

Hello, Wisdom

In *Tales for the Perfect Child* by Florence Parry Heide, there is a story about a little girl named Harriet who has perfected whining. She is described at being very skilled at it: "She practiced and practiced, and so of course she got better and better at it. Practice makes perfect." In the story Harriet decides that she wants a piece of blueberry pie. Her mother is fixing dinner and guests are coming soon. No matter. Harriet whines and whines because, as we all know, "good whiners make it hard for anyone to think of anything else." Good whiners stick to one subject. They don't give up. She gets her piece of pie.[3]

Practicing concentration is sort of like learning how to hone the art of the perfect whine, not that I would wish whining on anyone. The construct of a child's whine has much to teach us. It isn't personal. There isn't an assumed time limit. It takes a lot of energy. The energy doesn't decrease. If anything, the energy of a good whine increases with time. Outside factors like the weather, strangers who may have stopped to stare, or changes of place are irrelevant. With practice it is perfected.

Genuine concentration has similar attributes. It isn't connected to anything that is personal. A time limit isn't implied. It takes a significant amount of energy. Factors outside of what is being concentrated on become no more than a backdrop. It gets better with practice. It gets better when we refuse to give up. Over time, as we become increasingly skilled, wisdom arises. It shows up as a knowingness. We discover that we know exactly what is going on in the life situations we find ourselves in, both what is obvious and what is not so apparent. We understand what our function is in each situation, and we are able to respond in a way that doesn't harm. Underlying everything is a sweet feeling of okayness with all of it. Happy? Okay. Sad? Okay again. It feels weird at first, this wisdom. If you are anything like me, always the skeptic, you may tiptoe around it at first. But then, as you start to follow the instructions of this impersonal impulse as it pops up, your actions speak for themselves. Things play out in sweeter, more genuine, and less harmful ways—whether you've just had words with a cashier who has tried to scam your gift card or have to sit down to wrestle some relationship issues to the floor with your partner, who decided not to talk to you for the last four days.

As we learn to lean into wisdom, we discover that it is unfathomably comforting. And as long as we continue to be upright with our spiritual practice—following the eightfold path or its equivalent—wisdom is always there. We get the piece of pie. On the other hand, if we slack off (I speak from sad and pathetic experience here), letting our concentration muscles atrophy, wisdom erodes as well. We aren't as sharp. We don't notice as much. Our old, destructive habits, the ones that used to corner us into loser behavior, resurface and work their other-than-magic. Fortunately the discomfort that all of this creates typically leads us back to concentration practice, and wisdom. May the damage done in the meantime be small and easily erased.

There is another aspect of this wisdom that makes it worth the effort called for in concentration practice. We become kinder to ourselves. Every Asian monk I have ever spoken with at some length has commented on how harshly we westerners judge ourselves. We excel at it. Not thin enough. Not clever enough. Not active enough. Not mated. Not mated well. Not debt free. This harshness is powerful and habitual. With the wisdom that comes with concentration a funny thing happens to all of these judgments. They dissipate. We tell ourselves that it is okay that we made that mistake. That we are lovely in the body we have. That our debt problems have more to do with the larger economy than our own spending habits. That our mate is a genuinely good person. That everyone snores, lies sometimes, pretends, gets lazy, burns dinner. Okay. Because our judgment habits are so ingrained, it can help to have something close at hand that can trigger a softer and more genuine acceptance of ourselves just the way we are. A meditation on loving-kindness is one example of something small that can have a huge impact on how we see ourselves and the world. Here is a version that was sent to me by one of my dharma sisters. I read it daily:

A Meditation on Loving-Kindness

If anyone has hurt me or harmed me knowingly or unknowingly in thought, word, or deed, I forgive

them. And I too ask for forgiveness if I have hurt any-
one or harmed anyone knowingly or unknowingly in
thought, word, or deed.
May I be happy.
May I be peaceful.
May I be free.
May my friends be happy.
May my friends be peaceful.
May my friends be free.
May my enemies be happy.
May my enemies be peaceful.
May my enemies be free.
May all beings be happy.
May all beings be peaceful.
May all beings be free.

Even just copying this meditation down on paper can be helpful.
Although the shifts in our lives caused by wisdom can be subtle, they are real. We may find that we're giving ourselves genuine
complements. We may hear ourselves quickly owning up to a mistake instead of rationalizing it away so as to lay the blame at someone else's feet. We may find ourselves actually scrubbing down the
laundry room instead of waving a soapy rag over its surfaces. These
are all examples of clues that concentration practice is working its
magic. We realize that even though we are, each one of us, no more
than dust motes, with all sorts of less-than-perfect eccentricities,
we are at the same time capable of manifesting a genuine wisdom
to offer the world.

Beau, now almost four, appears at the front door. He is here for a play date of supper, stories, and movies. He wants cookies first. I look at him. He looks at me. I ask him, "Is your name Harriet?" He nods yes. "Well then, Harriet, do you commit to eating three pieces of broccoli, one half of a garden burger, and six rice chips after the cookie?" Another affirmative.

"Let's do it."

We each eat a cookie. I dip mine in some almond milk. Then we each eat three pieces of broccoli, a half of a garden burger, and six rice chips without any whining from either of us. Then we clean the kitchen, top to bottom. Just because. We sit down together on the couch to SpongeBob SquarePants, laughing during breaks and telling each other stories. I love him and want him to experience the happiness I feel when we are together. Sitting with him, it occurs to me that this is exactly what the bodhisattva vow is all about. We want everyone to feel this happiness. Everyone. And we want to do whatever we can to make this possible, even if it means watching the same SpongeBob SquarePants episode for the twelfth time.

THE POWER OF PERSEVERANCE

Jamie has decided to do the Couch-to-5K running plan. At almost thirty, she wants to be more fit. Also she is a bridesmaid in a wedding in three months. She wants a tighter body. Even though she is genuinely beautiful, I understand her motivation. The dresses are yellow. Her boyfriend will be there. I've already seen the power of this program to turn couch potato television/Internet lovers into people who miss going outside for some exercise a couple of times a week, even in the worst weather.

The reason the program works is not because it boot-camps you into becoming a marathon runner. It works because it relies on perseverance. Beginners are encouraged to ease into the program gradually. Each combination of walking and jogging should only take about a half hour, and you are encouraged not to do the program more than three times a week, spacing out the days to give your body a break. You aren't even supposed to be able to run three miles before two months is up.

Here are a couple of examples of the schedule:

Week One: Workout One: Brisk 5-minute warm-up walk. Then alternate 60 seconds of jogging and 90 seconds of walking, for a total of 20 minutes.

Week Five: Workout One: Brisk 5-minute warm-up walk, then jog 5 minutes, walk 3 minutes, jog 5 minutes, walk 3 minutes, jog 5 minutes.

People who have completed the program warn newbies not to get impatient or to skip ahead. The trick is just to stick to what feels sort of easy and very doable while your body calibrates itself to the shifting you: "Don't try to do more, even if you feel you can. . . . Don't feel pressured to continue faster than you're able. Repeat weeks if needed and move ahead only when you feel you're ready."[4] So three days a week Jamie and her housemate plan to simply show up until, at some point, their bodies will urge them to get off the couch and start running—and they'll want to.

Growing our concentration muscles works exactly the same way. The point isn't to power our way into extremely concentrated states. The point is to keep showing up. How? By paying attention to what is right in front of us. When we turn on our attention headlight, we quickly see how well we're concentrating on whatever we're doing. Mostly we aren't. Mostly we're bouncing all over the place, from planning to remembering to fantasizing. There isn't anything wrong with this. On the other hand, just like the Couch-to-5K program, if we keep showing up to practice concentrating, at some point it will start to kick in on its own. Maybe we'll suddenly notice that we're washing the dishes simply to wash the dishes. Or we actually make it most of the way through a period of meditation without mentally writing up the week's list of chores that need doing.

Concentration is a muscle that strengthens with practice. When we persevere by bringing our minds back again and again to what is right here it gives us enormous gifts. We notice more. Appreciate more. Boredom becomes impossible. Our lives become more balanced. We see that every day is its own wonderland. Without meaning to, we become more loving and kind and open to others. We notice when someone needs us to be quiet or to call them. After a while, like the running plan, concentration becomes its own motivation.

The catch, and there is one, is that like the Couch-to-5K program, we never know when concentration will kick itself in. This means that those of us who put a deadline on our enlightenment (I gave myself a year) are pretty much doomed. Most people who have benefited from perseverance admit that they've had to keep going well beyond any self-imposed deadline. In my fifth year of meditation practice, I can remember sitting myself down and saying, "P'arang, you need to make the 10,000-year commitment." I had been practicing hard, including living in two Buddhist temples. And I had noticed that I was definitely calmer and coping more skillfully with my chaotic life. On the other hand, my neurotic tendencies are deep and tangled, and if there is anything that neurotic tendencies love, it's a cleared out mind space to fill. It probably took another five years before I could sit quietly without a ticker tape of thinking showing up. I've learned that all of these conditioned habits that want to separate me from "just this" continue to need some serious unraveling. While this has meant that I've needed to make the 10,000-year vow more than I ever thought I would, the years of perseverance have nevertheless led to a deeply changed life—a happy one, no matter what. All these many years later I am pleased to report that a morning meditation is now as natural and quiet as one could ever hope for, with smatterings of monkey mind at the beginning of almost every sitting just to keep me honest. Next up? Getting off the couch to train for a 5K if Jamie will have me.

Moving Past Bliss

My friend Alan tells a wonderful story about three wise men searching for the ring of happiness. They have heard that one exists from an old woman known for her wisdom. When she tells them that the ring can humble the rich in a way that will make them happy even if they lose their riches, they are goners. Nothing like a guarantee to motivate treasure hunts. At first they focus on fancy, expensive rings, but when nothing happens as they try them on, they start looking for the not-so-fancy kind. Finally, one of the wise men spots an old copper ring—probably the last ring in the kingdom, given how these stories go. When he sees it, at first he almost ignores it. A simple copper ring, after all. Kind of dirty. But he picks it up and looks it over. When he looks at the inside he smiles. "This is it." Inside there is an inscription: "This too shall pass."

Bliss hits most of us by surprise. We're tooling along, meditating away, or chanting, or praying, and suddenly we're smack in the middle of a fabulous rainbow world. We realize that we're exactly where we should be, doing exactly what we should be doing. We're in love with everything and everyone. We suddenly understand the expression "shiny eyes" because we can literally feel an intensity resting behind our own eyes. It feels like the sun wanting to shine out instead of in.

Shakyamuni Buddha struck the bliss lode early on in his practice. When he was a boy he had a wonderful experience of quiet bliss when he was sitting under a tree watching his father work his fields. Later, when he first decided to formally become a mendicant, he studied under two yogis known for their ability to tap into the blissful state and then some. In Buddha's day, as far as all the ascetics were concerned they had reached the apex of spiritual maturity.

The problem was, and still is, that bliss doesn't eradicate suffering and its causes. So, just like Buddha, when we come back out of the clouds, and we all do, we discover that our own versions of greed, anger, and delusion have been patiently waiting for our return. So we haven't become more advanced after all. We've just had a break—one for the history books, maybe—from our own personalized hell realm, the one where we still worry, backbite, get jealous, and feel sorry for ourselves.

This is good to remember. Here's why: For many people, bliss becomes its own false god. It feels so good that we want more. Because we want more we may decide to learn from teachers who have their bliss on fairly constantly. If they can, we can. We admire them, put them on pedestals, and imitate them. We imagine that all their negative emotions have dissipated into the ether, and that ours will, too. Except that all the dreck, theirs and ours, hasn't gone anywhere. Instead, unmonitored, things can get worse. We forget to pay attention, to trust our own instincts. The bliss is just too seductive. This is when teachers and ministers can forget their ethics and abuse their power. At best, students are led up an impermanent tree with promises of more and more bliss. If we're lucky, our fall from bliss will be fast and not too far.

When we do fall, most of us want to throw the baby out with the bath water. At least I did. We paint our former teachers as evil incarnate, when most of them are simply doing their job. They are teaching what they were taught. At the time of our fall, though, none of this matters. We are heartbroken. If, instead of running completely away, we can back up to a simple practice of meditation or prayer in a place that is safe for us, we will discover that somehow the experience of bliss has made it easier for us to sit in calm abiding. From here we then see the work we need to do for ourselves, by ourselves—working with impatience or laziness or anger or a sense of self-importance. Right here is where concentration can step in as a great healer. If we stay focused on our basic practice, gently and quietly, aspects of our lives that make us crazy stop. Not that the things themselves necessarily stop, but the craziness does. We're wiser. We've learned to discriminate. We've let go of the need to be, or follow, anyone who is special. All we need to keep going is to continue to concentrate on whatever needs doing, moment by moment. As we do, we further discover that, all by ourselves, we really are bodhisattvas through and through. And we can be of service to the world in ways that the world needs.

7: Equanimity

....

Just as an elephant in a battlefield
endures the arrows shot from a bow,
I too will endure abuse.
Indeed, many people in this world
harm.
. . .
There is no mode of transportation
that can take a person
to Nirvana.
Only by controlling one's senses
and training one's mind
can that goal be reached.
—THE STILL POINT DHAMMAPADA[1]

....

BUDDHA AND HIS GOOD FRIEND DRUNK ELEPHANT

ONE OF THE more entertaining stories in Buddha's life was his interaction with a drunken elephant. His cousin Devadatta, who was prone to jealousy and wanting to kill Buddha, got an elephant drunk, and when Buddha and his followers came into town,

Devadatta let the animal loose. It stormed down the main street, straight at the crowd. People were so terrified that they leapt out of the way, except for Buddha and his attendant, Ananda, who was probably too terrified to react. The Buddha waited until the elephant was about to plow into him. Then he put his hand out, at which point the elephant fell to the ground, as docile as a puppy. The alcohol was no match for the peaceful state that is Buddha.

I have been thinking about this story a lot lately. I come from a long line of alcoholics. My father was one. My son is one, albeit a sober one, as I write. That I don't care for its taste is probably the only reason I haven't joined our family's cadre of AA members. Even so, this family trait has made me hypersensitive to all things alcoholic, mostly because I see how the behavior blocks equanimity in all its forms.

We all have addictions. I've lived long enough, and been a minister long enough, to believe that this is simply part of being human. We're going to be addicted to some things. It's just how it is. I, for one, am completely addicted to human life. I love waking up each morning to a new day, thrilled that we haven't been hit by an asteroid (as you know). Life means puppy licks and long walks by the river and a family that, even in the throes of great melodrama, loves me. At the same time I'm also addicted to sugar and frozen chocolate cake. It is hard to imagine ever tiring of either of these.

And yet.

It turns out that some addictions harm faster, harder, and longer than others. Buddha singled out alcohol consumption as a serious roadblock for spiritual seekers. He didn't start out that way. But then, one of the kings of his time, King Udena of Vamsa, changed everything. Udena was so mad about all the alms-begging monks who kept showing up for water and food that he gave an order to put palm wine in all the water jars that were typically left around the city for mendicants. You can just imagine the result—drunk monks everywhere. Naked, drunken monks. When Buddha showed up to see if the rumors of drunken dancing monks were true, he found one of his senior disciples splayed out on the ground, passed out from too much alcohol.

Horrified, and unhappy that he couldn't get a promise from the king to put water in the jugs, Buddha issued an order prohibiting monks from drinking alcohol. He never waivered from that prohibition; later he further instructed that any monk who drank would be prohibited from being ordained. Addiction to alcohol is such an issue in the Buddhist tradition that one of the precepts, or vows, that many of us make when we formally sign up for this path is to refrain from intoxicants.

A tall order. But history has taught us that addictions are harmful. They may start and end with alcohol, but there is a whole universe of problematic yearnings in between. It is always the right time to take a personal inventory to see what needs work, knowing that with addictions we'll probably be falling on our faces many times before any real change happens. But just owning up to an addiction is not only an important first step but the only gate that can potentially free us from the pull of whatever we're craving. In Zen we have a helpful saying: "Nine times fall down, ten times get up." In my case the falling and getting up pattern is more like fall down twice a day, get up three times. Every day. Then change happens, but only when I continue to admit to the problem and only when I'm willing to try, try, try. I've noticed that when spiritual practice is strong, sugar has little pull, and I forget about the chocolate cake in the freezer. Why? Because moment to moment this life rocks. The trees. The smells. The colors. The hummingbird looking at the penstemon for any new blooms. The cat sitting on my lap for once. Even when it's fleeting, this equanimity is well worth giving up the cravings.

There is a wonderful story from the life of Mahatma Gandhi that is useful as an incentive to keep trying, trying, trying when it comes to addictions. It seems that one of his followers had a son who was obsessed with eating sugar. His mother was so undone by his behavior that she made the boy walk with her to seek Gandhi's advice. We're talking walking miles under a scorching sun, here. When they got to Gandhi and told him the predicament, he asked them to come back in two weeks. Confused and not a little annoyed, they headed home and then returned a few weeks later. When they met with Gandhi the second time, the mother asked him why they had to wait for his advice. His response? "Sister, two weeks ago I too was eating a lot of sugar. You must be the change you wish to see in the world."

Nothing Gets Rewarded

I first heard about the filmmaker Michael Moore when I moved to Flint, Michigan, as a young PhD. The city, birthplace to General Motors, had been decimated by the loss of the company, its suppliers, and various plants associated with both. You could play soccer on Saginaw Street, the main drag, without worrying about running into any traffic—in the middle of the day. What was weird about living there for a newcomer like me was that the place is actually beautiful. A lovely, small river courses through the middle of downtown, and the city is surrounded by fresh lakes and farmland. The downtown buildings have obviously been designed by some of the world's finest architects. Nonetheless, and in spite of the millions of dollars that the C.S. Mott Foundation was investing in the city annually, the place was a handful of buildings away from being a complete ghost town—all because of the loss of GM.

Michael, through a newspaper he started with some friends called *The Flint Voice*, was the lone public voice that went after the corruption he saw in local politicians. He believed they were still pandering to corporate interests. He also went after the less than ethical behavior he saw happening in the auto industry, going on to make a quirky documentary, *Roger and Me*, about the corruption within General Motors in particular. The film is both hilarious and heartbreaking and did what no other public forum had been able to pull off to date—it gave the rest of us real data we could use to decide for ourselves how we felt about the automotive industry. From there, Michael went on to take on the George W. Bush presidency and the health care industry with the same combination of fact, story, and humor. Whatever one might think of him personally, I have no doubt that his intentions were honorable. Through the vehicle of entertainment, where humor can make it possible for us to hear what we otherwise might ignore, Michael wanted to show the truth of the corruption of power in its various forms— how it happens and how it hurts. His team has always been open about the research they have done and have been willing to have it double-checked.

The reward for all of this effort? Michael Moore is second only to the president of the United States in the number of serious death threats (about 450) he has received. They are serious enough to have led to his hiring nine former Navy Seals to protect him and his family. All he wanted to do was tell the truth about institutions that are harming us. I am guessing that the death threats aren't the reward he expected.

One of the first expressions I came across when I first started meditating was "expect no reward." I remember thinking that such a phrase is about the worst thing you could say to a newbie meditator. We want rewards. Actually we want more than that. We all want gains, yes, but we also want praise, a good reputation, and pleasure. We don't want loss, blame, bad reputations, or pain. We don't want to have to hire Navy Seals to protect our families.

The problem is that each of us gets all these things. For every gain, there is loss. While we may be praised one minute, I guarantee that blame will be right around the corner. A good reputation can shift to a bad one in the blink of an eye. We all know pain, and while we may not need bodyguards, we all have someone who would be quite happy if we weren't alive. When I first started Still Point, an old Zen master told me that I wouldn't have earned my dharma teacher stripes until someone started to spread meanspirited and untrue rumors about me. It took about six weeks.

Nobody signs up for the less than stellar consequences of practice when we first sit down on a cushion. We've come for calmness, after all—some sanity in a pretty crazy world. Instead what we get is a roller coaster. Calmness. Blame. Taking more responsibility for our actions. Getting blamed for things we had nothing to do with. Then we have to sit on a cushion and watch all the bouncy thinking that tries to make sense of it all. Weren't there going to be some rewards here? Even when bliss hits, it eventually goes. And our emerging psychic tendencies don't make the traffic any lighter or prevent our little sister from sneaking onto our private Facebook page, only to turn around to tell our parents everything.

It turns out that expecting no reward is a giant clue to how to successfully ride the waves of gain and loss that come with spiritual practice. When we just do the practice without expectations we discover an equanimity that has always been right there. This equanimity makes it possible to simply watch. We watch how long it takes for a negative emotion to quiet down. We watch how long we get caught by words of praise. We see the places where we can chip away at old karmic habits and yearnings. We figure out the personal antidotes to our strongest negative habits. We experience how simply owning up to the negativity allows it to wash away surprisingly quickly. We see where we might be needed in the world and how to get from our cushion to that place. Maybe this means becoming a master gardener in an inner city. Maybe it means being a great mom. Maybe it means guarding a truth teller so he can keep doing his work.

NOT RUNNING AWAY

Shakyamuni Buddha was a spoiled-brat rich kid. First off, he was born to elderly parents. His mother, Maya, and father, Suddhodana, not quite a king and queen but close, tried for years to have a child before his mother, at forty, became pregnant. Given that the average life span at the time (583 B.C.E.) was twenty-five, this was its own miracle.

Because his parents were good people, everyone in the Shakya clan was thrilled with their news. Suddhodana had a reputation for being a fair magistrate who knew "how to grow rice." There is no higher praise. All this meant that Shakyamuni, known by his birth name, Siddhartha Gotama, had everything he could ever wish for from his first breath. To make matters worse—or better, depending on your point of view—at his birth the community's best psychics were called in to predict his future. The most respected of these, Asita, broke down in tears when he saw the baby. Why? Because he saw a king so sublime that he was heartbroken that he wouldn't live long enough to experience his reign.

As is true with many psychic pronouncements, there was a catch. Asita said the kingship could go one of two ways. Siddhartha could well take over his father's position, something both his parents prayed for, or he could become a spiritual king. Suddhodana was so determined that his son would follow his footsteps that he had him cloistered. Although he had to stay in one of the family's three palaces, he was allowed everything else he wished for. This translated into days spent immersed in various pleasures while everyone around him worked, including his father. Although Siddhartha took a few breaks, like when he saved a swan that had been shot by his cousin Devadatta or when he was coached by his father on how to be a judge, mostly he got to spend his days however he liked.

When Siddhartha was sixteen his father decided that marrying him off to the prettiest girl in all the land might get him off his royal behind. Yosadara's father, having seen the spoiled rich kid in all his nonglory, wasn't so sure about the matchup. To determine if he was in any shape to be a husband, the fathers concocted a sort of mini Olympics, matching Siddhartha against all the other teenage boys in Magadha. Much to everyone's shock, Siddhartha won every event as well as the young lady's heart. Word has it that they lived happily ever after for about thirteen years—a long time by today's standards.

The trouble was that Siddhartha couldn't get past a feeling of dissatisfaction that seemed to haunt him. Musicians, dancing girls, star-filled nights, a beautiful loving wife, and a precious baby boy did nothing to ease the feeling. He decided to sneak out of the palace grounds to check out the larger world to discover what he was missing. What he found was sickness, old age, and death, three aspects of living that his father had been paying an entire city to hide from his son, fearing that knowing about them would encourage his son to become a monk. It turns out that Suddhodana was correct. In spite of his best efforts and generous bribes, the sightings made the young man all the more determined to find out the cause of suffering and how it could be eradicated.

For the next six years he followed a path of starvation, more sick people, more dead people, and more old people. His studies under the best teachers of the time didn't get him any closer to understanding the connection between suffering and happiness: "'This teaching does not lead to . . . calm, to knowledge, to awakening, to Nibbana. . . .' So then I had had enough of this teaching, rejected it and turned away."[2]

The young man went off on his own and was, as you may recall, terrified. First he focused on a form of asceticism where he nearly starved to death. Realizing that this did not get him any closer to understanding suffering and its causes, he relaxed his hold and simply sat under a tree to meditate. Happily, enlightenment happened—in four stages. Sense desires ceased, bringing him tranquility. Deep concentration led to equanimity. As the equanimity deepened, he realized that he was free from sorrow. At this point Siddhartha, now Buddha, had his own psychedelic trip down memory lane—a review of his last 100,000 lives. When the trip was over he declared, with the earth as his witness, that he had found the path out of suffering.

For the next forty-five years he taught that path. In it are a number of surprising punch lines. One is that the trick to dealing with suffering is to lean into it. Not only does running away not work, but our suffering will just follow us wherever we go. If instead we focus on it with everything we've got, we'll see that suffering grows out of our own grasping and craving. We'll also see that there is a way out of this corner and that the way has three components: morality, concentration, and wisdom. We are suffering. First we see it. Then we own it. At that point the magic can happen. Following the guidelines of the eightfold path, we transform our reaction. We take care to keep our speech about what is happening upright—refraining from lying, slander, insults, or frivolous chatter. We follow right action, taking care not to harm anyone involved in the situation. We stay centered, concentrating on what is right in front of us to make certain we aren't missing anything.

Wisdom about how to respond to all of it grows out of these things. We'll know exactly what we need to do. And what we need to do is never about running away. Smack dab in the middle of it all will be a feeling of equanimity. Underneath everything we'll know that we are absolutely A-OK. This is happiness, the happiness brought to each of us by a spoiled brat almost-king who wouldn't run away from the big questions.

NOT RUNNING AWAY, PART 2

When the liberation of mind by equanimity is developed . . .
no limiting action remains there . . . . This too is the path
to the company of Brahma.[3]

Shit happens. A few months ago my son drove into a tree. He was drunk. He totaled his wife's jeep. Luckily he walked away. Luckily he didn't harm anyone else. When, shocked by the event, I started to tell my friends and family about it, everyone had similar stories. One woman lost a daughter-in-law to a car accident. Another friend's son was killed by a drunken driver. What we all had in common was a shared yearning to run away from the nightmare. We all wanted to pretend that the event had never happened.

But it did. With more to come, it seems. If I've learned anything in this lifetime, it's that shit keeps happening whether we want it to or not. This is where equanimity plays a key role in keeping us all sane. Buddha taught that equanimity is not only key to processing our lives as they are but is an unfailing method for living through the crises we'll all experience. Every family has a drunk. Maybe it's addiction to alcohol. If not, it will be an addiction to drugs or porn or sweets or work or the Internet. Or maybe to youth. Every family will face heartbreaking deaths—a beloved uncle, a newborn baby, a little sister. We'll all get sick. We'll all die. If we pay attention to what helps us in these crises we'll see that our fearlessness in staying right in the middle of whatever is going on will build our capacity for equanimity, and vice versa.

Equanimity has its own built-in reward system: right action. In Korean Buddhism there is a famous story about this power of nonresistance. During one of the many times that the Japanese army invaded Korea, they went into the mountains to destroy the temples and scoop up any precious metals they could find. Typically the monks fled for their lives whenever they heard soldiers coming. At Pae Yop Sah Temple on Gu Wol Mountain, one old monk refused to run. When the soldiers saw him they rushed the old fellow, threatening to kill him on the spot if he didn't leave.

He wouldn't move.

When they jabbed him with sticks he wouldn't move.

When one of the soldiers fired a warning shot into the ceiling, same response. Not moving.

Finally a senior officer showed up. He leaned into the monk and asked him if he was afraid of dying. Nope.

The Japanese general in charge of the raid watched all this. When he saw the fearlessness of the old monk he apologized and ordered his soldiers to leave the temple grounds without taking anything.[4]

While it isn't as powerful as the monk's serenity, my mother's equanimity has helped each of her five children to move through numerous crises. Once upon a time I was married to a good man who sadly was addicted to rage. After years of tiptoeing around him, I called her for advice.

"I'll help you move."

I was terrified that he would kill me if he found out I was trying to leave. My mother told me to call her when he was going on a business trip. I did, and she moved me. I was so scared, my legs wouldn't hold me up. She went through my house with a team of movers, telling them what to take, and settled me into a safe apartment, all in twenty-four hours. The entire time she never said an unkind word about my husband, never said, "I told you so," never scolded me for my choice in a mate. She just moved me. When we were done she flew home to Massachusetts. Her calm made it possible for me to do what I needed to do to be safe.

A friend tells a story of how, as a young contractor, he got tangled up through no fault of his own with some bullies who had a penchant for wearing expensive, dark suits with darker shirts. At one point they ended up following him around everywhere. When he mentioned this to his mother, she insisted on riding shotgun in his truck. One time, when the bullies had him cornered, she asked him to stop the truck. She got out, went up to their car, and demanded that they roll down their windows. They did. This was a tiny middle-aged woman. She calmly told them that they needed to leave her son alone. He had done nothing to them. If they harmed him in any way, they would have her to contend with, and she would never ever leave them alone. Then she calmly got back into my friend's truck and asked him to take her home. He was never followed again.

Equanimity makes it possible to put a situation on pause for long enough to see exactly what we need to do right now. My son found a sponsor and started going to AA meetings the morning following his accident. He contacted all his family members to profoundly apologize to each of us. He vowed to be a better husband and father. In return, I made a vow not to try to escape the heartbreak, the anger, and my fear of a recurrence. I vowed to continue to love him and to be helpful to him and his family without getting in the way of the reparations he is making. And every day I chant for all the families who have had to face something like this. In other words, I chant for all of us.

MELODRAMA WITHDRAWAL

The young man sitting across from me is gorgeous—dark-eyed and golden-skinned. He could definitely play the role of Shakyamuni Buddha the next time someone decides to film his life. He is unhappy—tear-filled-eyes unhappy. I'm a little surprised because I don't really know him outside of the zendo. I ask him how I can help. It turns out that his partner of several years has left him. He tells me it's his own fault.

"He told me I'm a drama queen. He's right. I am."

I find it hard to believe, but then I've only meditated with him. When I ask for examples he has plenty. Tantrums over small slights. Publicly teasing his partner, and not in a good way. A list of grudges as long as his very long arm. Just hearing about it makes my heart heavy. Reflecting on my own reactions to my partner's occasional misadventures, I think to myself, we're all melodrama queens.

He wants his partner back. He's tired of the drama. He wants to feel clear and calm when shit hits his fan. He wants a taste of equanimity. "Me too," I tell him. Will meditation help? It will, but it's a slow process. Think of a river that is moving so slowly that you can't see any ripples. It is definitely moving, but it takes a while to really see it.

"Is there anything else?"

I tell him that I've recently refamiliarized myself with the Alcoholics Anonymous Twelve-Step Program. That might work. We consider it together.

Step One: "We admitted we were powerless over alcohol—that our lives had become unmanageable." His experience? Everything feels like a crisis when it doesn't go his way. I know the feeling.

Step Two: "Came to believe that a Power greater than ourselves could restore us to sanity." Our take: Nobody is doomed to being a melodrama queen. The Buddha taught that everything arises and everything ceases. He didn't say most things. Trusting this teaching enough to give up the sense of doom may be pushing things, but there's nothing to lose in the trying.

Step Three: "Made a decision to turn our will and our lives over to the care of God as we understood Him." Our response: We both frown. This one is harder. The Buddha had no patience for questions about God, I tell him. On the other hand every Buddhist tradition that I can think of has some being they chant to for help when there is a crisis or in times of heartbreak. In the Korean tradition we chant to Quanseum Posal, the Bodhisattva of Great Compassion, all the time. The sangha is rife with stories of how this has been helpful, from one friend finding his way out of a Canadian forest to a group of monks chanting their empty gas tanked car all the way to a gas station. One of my dharma brothers, chanting in Seoul, completely broke, was helped by a parade of strangers until he was able to piece together financing for a plane ride home to the United States.

Step Four: "Made a searching and fearless moral inventory of ourselves." I shared with my young friend that in Buddhism the eightfold path offers a proven mirror where we can see our thoughts, words, and actions reflected back at us. This path specifically asks us not to harm in how we speak, act, and work. Melodrama harms in all three places. We cringe together. Apart from theatrical performances, I have never seen someone respond positively to melodramatic behavior on the part of someone else. At best, we're uncomfortable. At worst, we run away from whatever the relationship was; we rush to safety.

Step Five: "Admitted to God, to ourselves, and to another human being the exact nature of our wrongs." In Zen, serious practitioners admit to mistakes early and often. There is just no room for false anything. Humans make mistakes. We own ours and move on. Ironically this confession, often done out loud and in a public service, can put a powerful damper on melodrama, because just describing our actions out loud tends to make us careful not to repeat them.

Step Six: "Were entirely ready to have God remove all these defects of character." The eureka here for both of us was the acknowledgement that things don't have to be this way. Being a drama queen is always a choice. On this, the Buddha taught that there are four kinds of clinging that get us into serious trouble: clinging to sensual pleasures, clinging to views, clinging to rules and observances, and clinging to a doctrine of self. Melodrama encompasses at least three of these forms of clinging. When we're caught in it, we're hanging on to our views of how things should be, we're clinging to our take on the story, and we're clinging to our image of ourselves as supreme judges of all that surrounds us.

Step Seven: "Humbly asked Him to remove our shortcomings." I was raised to be feistily independent. Raising two kids a thousand miles away from any extended family taught me self-reliance, big S, big R. I just didn't ask people for help. When I moved to Detroit though, it became clear from day one that there was no way a single person could start a sangha in such an intense urban community without serious help. So I asked and was astonished at the support that showed up for Still Point (and still does). My biggest lesson came when a former student, beloved by all of us, killed himself. For the first time I understood the expression "crazy with grief." One night I couldn't cry hard enough to keep up with the heartbreak and literally threw myself onto the ground in front of the big Buddha statue in the meditation hall: "Please help."

In an instant I was calmer. The room felt bright and spacious and filled with what I can only call unending loving-kindness. I half expected that if I turned around I'd see our friend's ghost, the energy of the room was so different. I didn't have the guts to turn around. But I sat all night and by the next day had a grip on my mourning.

Step Eight: "Made a list of all persons we had harmed, and became willing to make amends to them." I told my tea-drinking companion that I've made this list several times. It is humbling and a terrific incentive for giving up the melodrama and whatever else is driving us to act like a jerk.

Step Nine: "Made direct amends to such people whenever possible, except when to do so would injure them or others." He said, "What do you think of a banner that says, 'I'm sorry I've been so fucking melodramatic'"? I replied that I didn't think it would be obvious who made the banner. But that might be a good thing. If everyone reading it thought it came from someone who had harmed them, the banner might mark the beginning of something big: universal forgiveness.

Step Ten: "Continued to take personal inventory and when we were wrong promptly admitted it." Back to the river. Even though change can be slow, it happens. For some reason, when I meditate in the mornings, screw-ups that need addressing pop up regularly. I've become skilled at sincere apologies and figuring out appropriate amends.

Step Eleven: "Sought through prayer and meditation to improve our conscious contact with God, as we understood Him, praying only for knowledge of His will for us and the power to carry that out." In Zen this is the miracle step. With meditation practice we understand more and more what every single situation needs us to do. It's uncanny. God or no God, this understanding happens to everyone's benefit.

Step Twelve: "Having had a spiritual awakening as the result of these Steps, we tried to carry this message to alcoholics, and to practice these principles in all our affairs."

The bodhisattva vow: All beings, one body, I vow to liberate. Endless blind passions I vow to uproot. Dharma gates without number I vow to penetrate. The great way of Buddha I vow to attain.

I'd like to tell you that the Twelve-Step Program worked miracles for my young friend and that he got his partner back. The truth is that I have no idea what happened to him. He may have written me off as a crazy woman willing to buy tea for anyone wanting advice. What I do know is that just talking about the program's steps calmed him considerably. His shoulders relaxed. He leaned in. He smiled. It was a start.

How To Be a Seamless Monument

Sarah is twenty-five years younger than I am, to the day. I see her twice a week at a Nia dance class. I discovered Nia years ago in Ann Arbor when I was walking past a recreation center on one of the city's side streets. It was the music—pounding world music. I followed it into a room crammed with moving bodies, mostly female. They seemed to be headed in every direction at once, working hard, grinning wide. At the time I was too busy to do anything more than gape. When I later moved to the northwest I discovered that Nia classes are taught everywhere here. The first class I tried was in Seattle. The teacher, introducing herself to the four of us who showed up for her class in a ballroom dance studio—complete with a huge disco ball over the middle of the parquet floor—wept as she told us that Nia saved her life. Disconcerted and not needing my life saved, I waited until I moved south to Eugene to try again.

Nia combines basic dance moves with yoga, martial arts, and tai chi. You never know what to expect in a class, because the routines change each time. You only know that the class will be a lot of fun and a terrific workout.

Sarah is beautiful, tall, and thin. She looks like a fairy princess, with her thick black curls, twinkling eyes, and wide smile. Mostly what she is is a skillful dance instructor—on every level. Almost every class starts out with some complaining on the part of several students. The room is too cold. It's too hot. There isn't enough air. There is too much air. Sarah always hears these out and does what she can to make us all comfortable. Sometimes the heat gets turned down. Sometimes she suggests that we keep our hoodies on until the room warms up from our efforts. Sometimes she opens one or two windows. After several years of taking classes from her I have yet to see a response of irritation, even though the truth of every class is that someone will complain about something.

Her other guaranteed reaction is one of great patience with the actual dancing that happens. Since each class has different routines and we don't learn them beforehand (this being the Nia way), we are forever making mistakes—jumping in the wrong direction, stretching when we should be moving into a restful pose, arriving and leaving whenever we like. No matter what, she is always ready to compliment and encourage. Last week only three of us made it to a class in the dead of winter (which actually isn't much to brag about in Eugene, but still). Sarah had us doing some complicated dance routines, and we were moving fast. At one point, watching us in the mirror at the room's front she exclaimed, "Beautiful, beautiful!" and obviously meant it. The thing is, we were all doing completely different dance steps. And we were all wrong! She didn't care. We were beautiful. And we felt beautiful reflected in her eyes.

There's an old Zen story about a master who is dealing with a student who is fussing about the master's dying. After the master dies, wails the student, what should he do? The master's response is that the student needs to build a seamless monument for him.

When I first heard this story I literally scratched my head in confusion. Another opaque Zen lesson. Didn't these guys have anything better to do than to sit around causing headaches for the rest of us? But then I considered it more deeply. Monuments always stand for something that is considered to be noble by the society that erects them. Their inscriptions are meaningful and virtually always call on us to be our best selves—to care about others and try to help. Here's an example from the Lincoln Monument in Washington, D.C.

"With malice toward none; with charity for all; with firmness in the right, as God gives us to see the right, let us strive on to finish the work we are in; to bind up the nation's wounds; to care for him who shall have borne the battle, and for his widow, and his orphan—to do all which may achieve and cherish a just and lasting peace, among ourselves, and with all nations."

But monuments have seams. That old trickster of a Zen master was telling his student to shape up and be a living monument himself—someone quick to compassion and kindness. Someone ready to help. Someone capable of seeing the innate and breathtaking beauty in everything and everyone. Someone like Sarah.

Conclusion

ZEN BUDDHISM OFFERS a universe of practices, all aimed at opening our minds and hearts. The seven factors of enlightenment, when we give ourselves over to them, act like oil poured onto a spiritual brush fire. They bring our spiritual effort home to what is, so we can become what the world needs us to be. Each factor has the capacity to manifest in countless shapes, styles, and situations. The fun part is that we get to see clearly what our versions are of each factor. Working with the messiness entailed in all this work leads us to lose our innocence. We trade it in for wonder.

The main thing to remember along the way is that our life is what our mind makes it out to be. We always get to choose. In a famous story about Hakuin, one of Zen's great patriarchs, a samurai comes to him for a teaching. He wants to know the difference between heaven and hell. Hakuin's response? "You dumb-ass!"

The samurai is immediately pissed beyond belief. "I'll kill you!"

Hakuin looks at him. "That's hell."

The samurai freezes in place. Then he bows to the old monk.

"That's heaven," Hakuin says.

In the end we have to work on our mind alone. It is solitary work. Wise words can only encourage us to keep going. On the other hand we can use the teachings to see where we need to scrub hard. And then we can scrub. If you are feeling unsure about where to begin, simply sit quietly, thinking about the seven factors of enlightenment. Then ask yourself this question: "Where do I need to focus?"

I guarantee a response will pop up. For me it almost always has to do with mindfulness. I still have a tendency to rush through my days, missing a myriad of opportunities to take refuge in the uprightness of "just this." In the West, where we all seem to share a cultural tendency to busy up our days, considering the factors even if just for a few moments has a way of bringing our energy back to where it needs to be. Cooking a healthy breakfast. Cleaning the bedroom. Listening to our partner. Feeding the baby. Weeping with our dying friend. Laughing ourselves hoarse at Stephen Colbert's interview with Maurice Sendak.

On a pilgrimage to Japan, Peter Matthiessen, a longtime student of Zen and the author of *Nine-Headed Dragon River*, had a rare opportunity to visit one of his root teachers, Soen Nakagawa. They had been to hell and back together, building a temple in the United States, living through the death of Peter's wife, and experiencing years of separation when Soen removed himself to a small, isolated hermitage in Japan following years of teaching.

When they took leave of each other for the final time, Soen looked at Peter and told him to take good care of himself. After all their years as student and teacher, a simple sentiment. In that sentence is a blessing and an instruction. Do your work. Be kind to yourself while you do it. Be your own Buddha. Trust. His words convey a universe of kindness. In that moment, nothing separated the two. Heaven.

Take good care of yourself.

September 17, 2012, Eugene, Oregon.

May all beings be free.

Notes

CHAPTER 1

1. Seung Sahn, *The Compass of Zen* (Boston: Shambhala, 1997), 102.
2. Bhikkhu Bodhi, ed., *In the Buddha's Words: An Anthology of Discourses from the Pali Canon* (Boston: Wisdom, 2005), 239–40.
3. Sakyong Mipham, "Let It Shine!" *Shambhala Sun*, Nov. 2011, 18.
4. H. W. Schumann, *The Historical Buddha: The Times, Life and Teachings of the Founder of Buddhism* (New York: Arkana, 1989), 50.
5. S. N. Goenka, "Pure Attention," *Buddhadharma: The Practitioner's Quarterly*, Spring 2003, 2.
6. Seung Sahn, *Compass of Zen*, 103.
7. Bhikkhu Bodhi, *Buddha's Words*, 392.
8. Quoted in Eilene Zimmerman, "Distracted? It's Time to Hit the Reset Button," *New York Times*, Nov. 20, 2011.
9. Bhikkhu Bodhi, *Buddha's Words*, 33–34.

CHAPTER 2

1. Robert Buswell Jr., trans., *The Korean Approach to Zen: The Collected Works of Chinul* (Honolulu: University of Hawaii Press, 1983), 62.
2. Peter Mayle, *Where Did I Come From?* (New York: Lyle Stuart, 1977), unpaged.
3. Buswell, *Korean Approach to Zen*, 138.
4. Bhikkhu Bodhi, *Buddha's Words*, 83.
5. Frank Bruni, "In Praise of Borders," *New York Times*, October 30, 2011.
6. Seung Sahn, *The Whole World Is a Single Flower: 365 Kong-ans for Everyday Life* (Boston: Tuttle, 1992), 12–13.
7. Bhikkhu Bodhi, *Buddha's Words*, 400.
8. Seung Sahn, *Compass of Zen*, 369.
9. John Daido Loori, *The Zen of Creativity: Cultivating Your Artistic Life* (New York: Ballantine, 2004), 52.

CHAPTER 3

1. Schumann, *Historical Buddha*, 250.

2. Maurice Walshe, trans., *The Long Discourses of the Buddha: A Translation of the Digha Nikaya* (Boston: Wisdom, 1995), 125.

3. Ibid., 129–31.

4. Eido Shimano, "Joshu's Mu," in *The Book of Mu: Essential Writings on Zen's Most Important Koan*, eds. James Ishmael Ford and Melissa Myozen Blacker (Boston: Wisdom, 2011), 133.

5. Walshe, *Long Discourses of Buddha*, 219.

6. Ibid., 233.

7. Thomas Cleary, trans., *Book of Serenity* (Boston: Shambhala, 1998), 108.

8. Bhikkhu Bodhi, *Buddha's Words*, 170.

CHAPTER 4

1. Geri Larkin, *The Still Point Dhammapada: Living the Buddha's Essential Teachings* (HarperSanFrancisco, 2003), 88.

2. Bhikkhu Bodhi, *Buddha's Words*, 26.

3. Schumann, *Historical Buddha*, 53.

4. Seung Sahn, *Compass of Zen*, 349.

5. Walshe, *Discourses of the Buddha*, 386; 388.

6. Ibid., 389.

7. Schumann, *Historical Buddha*, 148–49.

CHAPTER 5

1. Larkin, *Still Point Dhammapada*, 102–03.

2. Bunno Kato, Yoshiro Tamura, and Kojiro Miyasaka, trans., *The Threefold Lotus Sutra* (Tokyo: Kosei Publishing, 1975), 177.

3. Bhikkhu Bodhi, *Buddha's Words*, 116.

4. Ibid., 117

CHAPTER 6

1. Bhikkhu Bodhi, *Buddha's Words*, 303.

2. Walshe, *Discourses of the Buddha*, 297.

3. Florence Parry Heide, *Tales for the Perfect Child* (New York: Dell, 1985), 55; 58.

4. Josh Clark, "The Couch-to-5K Running Plan," Feb. 6, 2012, http://www.coolrunning.com/engine/2/2_3/181.shtml.

CHAPTER 7

1. Larkin, *Still Point Dhammapada*, 163–64.

2. Schumann, *Historical Buddha*, 48.

3. Bhikkhu Bodhi, *Buddha's Words*, 178.

4. Seung Sahn, *Compass of Zen*, 202.

About the Author

THE DAUGHTER of an IBM engineer and a wildly brilliant artist, Geri Larkin grew up in various cities in the United States and in Sydney, Australia. After earning a doctorate in policy analysis, she joined Deloitte as a management consultant in 1988. Larkin attended the Maitreya Buddhist Seminary from 1992 to 1995, when she was ordained as a dharma teacher. In 1999 she started Still Point Zen Buddhist Temple in the heart of Detroit, where she was guiding teacher for its first five years. Larkin is the author of seven books on Buddhism, including *Stumbling Toward Enlightenment* and *The Still Point Dhammapada,* and writes a regular column for *Spirituality & Health.* These days she lives in Eugene, Oregon, where she volunteers, babysits, writes, cleans, and practices as much as possible, given that there aren't many years left.

All author royalties will be donated to the Eugene Right Livelihood Fund.

About the Publisher

SHAMBHALA PUBLICATIONS is pleased to publish the Rodmell Press collection of books on yoga, Buddhism, and aikido. As was the aspiration of the founders of Rodmell Press, it is our hope that these books will help individuals develop a more skillful practice—one that brings peace to their daily lives and to the Earth.

To learn more, please visit www.shambhala.com.

Index

Printed in the United States
By Bookmasters